Socialization of Graduate and Professional Students in Higher Education

A Perilous Passage?

John C. Weidman, Darla J. Twale, Elizabeth Leahy Stein

ASHE-ERIC Higher Education Report Volume 28, Number 3
Adrianna J. Kezar, Series Editor

Prepared and published by

 **JOSSEY-BASS**
A Wiley Company
San Francisco

In cooperation with

ERIC Clearinghouse on Higher Education
The George Washington University
URL: www.eriche.org

Association for the Study
of Higher Education
URL: www.tiger.coe.missouri.edu/~ashe

Graduate School of Education and Human Development
The George Washington University
URL: www.gwu.edu

Socialization of Graduate and Professional Students in Higher Education: A Perilous Passage?
John C. Weidman, Darla J. Twale, Elizabeth Leahy Stein
ASHE-ERIC Higher Education Report Volume 28, Number 3
Adrianna J. Kezar, Series Editor

This publication was prepared partially with funding from the Office of Educational Research and Improvement, U.S. Department of Education, under contract no. ED-99-00-0036. The opinions expressed in this report do not necessarily reflect the positions or policies of OERI or the Department.

ISSN 0884-0040   ISBN 0-7879-5836-0

The ASHE-ERIC Higher Education Report is part of the Jossey-Bass Higher and Adult Education Series and is published six times a year by Jossey-Bass, 350 Sansome Street, San Francisco, California 94104-1342.

For subscription information, see the Back Issue/Subscription Order Form in the back of this journal.

Prospective authors are strongly encouraged to contact Adrianna Kezar, Director, ERIC Clearinghouse on Higher Education, at (202) 296-2597 ext. 14 or akezar@eric-he-edu.

Visit the Jossey-Bass Web site at **www.josseybass.com.**

Executive Summary

This report on the process of graduate and professional student socialization provides information that can be of use to graduate program faculty and administrators, professional associations, state legislatures, and professional licensing bodies charged with assuring clients that well qualified professional practitioners are being prepared in the nation's universities. It addresses implications of issues raised in the current literature for designing more effective graduate programs.

What Is Socialization in Graduate School?

Socialization in graduate school refers to the processes through which individuals gain the knowledge, skills, and values necessary for successful entry into a professional career requiring an advanced level of specialized knowledge and skills. The first two sections describe the various elements of this socialization process, drawing from research on adult socialization, role acquisition, and career development.

Four stages are identified in the socialization process: anticipatory, formal, informal, and personal. These stages reflect different levels of understanding and commitment to the professional roles for which graduate students are being prepared. Each stage involves a process of engagement through the core elements of socialization that lead to increasingly more advanced knowledge acquisition, involvement in the culture of the academic program, especially with faculty through mentoring and supervision of graduate students' work.

How Might a Schematic Representation of the Graduate and Professional Student Socialization Process Look?

A conceptual model of graduate and professional student socialization, adapted from a framework addressing socialization of undergraduates, is presented in the third section, "A Framework for the Socialization of Graduate and Professional Students." At the center of the model is the core socialization experience, consisting of the *normative context* (teaching, research, service) of the graduate academic program, *socialization processes* (interaction, integration, learning), and *core elements* (knowledge acquisition, investment, involvement).

Surrounding the center are the four other dimensions: *prospective students* (background, predisposition), *personal communities* (family, friends, employers), *professional communities* (practitioners, associations), and *novice professional practitioners* (commitment, identity). While all these elements exist to a significant extent outside the university setting, they have varying degrees of influence on academic programs and the graduate students enrolled in them.

The model assumes that socialization occurs through an interactive set of stages rather than in a linear manner that would associate each stage with a particular dimension in the model. Socialization processes characteristic of all four stages may be present simultaneously at any point in the entire graduate experience.

How Does a Socialization Perspective Help to Identify Changes That Should Be Considered to Develop More Effective Graduate Degree Programs?

The fourth section, "Institutional Culture: Recurrent Themes," illustrates several changing patterns in graduate education that are exerting pressure for reform, among them diversity, international students, professional preparation, ethics, use of technology, and student support. Also highlighted are some of the initiatives under way to improve the experience of graduate and professional students through program restructuring, including modifying faculty roles. Specific improvements in graduate programs advocated by major national commissions include developing greater flexibility in curriculum and requirements as well as more options for students so that graduates are more versatile and complete degrees in a more timely fashion, attracting more women and minority group members, providing better information about careers, training faculty to be better mentors, and providing more systematic supervision of graduate students' work.

It is incumbent upon faculty and practicing professionals to build academic programs that socialize graduate students through a continuous process from admission through entry into a professional role that is under constant review and modification. The ongoing interaction of faculty, graduate students, and professionals can provide effective avenues for responding to the changing requirements of a dynamic environment. Through collaboration, students and faculty can consciously and conscientiously sustain their community so that personal support, protection during experimentation and risk taking, and emotional security are encouraged. The graduate and professional socialization process should reflect expanding knowledge in the field of study, changing global trends, needs of increasingly diverse student populations, new technologies, and societal demands for the education of highly skilled professionals.

What Are the Differences in Students' Experiences Across Graduate Programs

Despite similarities between them, no two graduate and professional programs are identical, and no two students experience graduate or professional school in quite the same way. Programs that prepare students for careers in academe differ from professional programs that prepare students for nonacademic careers. Master's and professional degree programs are different from doctoral degree programs. And there are as many differences in content and approach across advanced academic and professional fields as there are within specific fields. Graduate students experience socialization processes that reflect their chosen discipline, the structure and sequence of their academic program, and their university setting.

The fifth section, "Institutional Culture and Socialization: Differences Among Academic Programs," contrasts socialization processes across academic program goals, faculty expectations, and student peer culture. Examining differences sets the stage for reflecting in the final section on how graduate education can be structured more effectively in ways that are sensitive to increasingly diverse groups of graduate students.

Contents

Foreword

Several reports predict the retirement of a large percentage of the professoriat over the next decade. Many departments are already experiencing vast turnover. In my own department, more than half the faculty retired during the past year. With this large turnover in faculty, every institution, school, and department needs to think about the education and socialization of graduate students.

Many new initiatives have been forged to improve the challenges of graduate education and socialization. One prominent effort to address the socialization of graduate students is the Preparing Future Faculty Project, aimed at educating the new cadre of professors about the range of institutional options, the diversity of the faculty role, and advice for a complex and demanding career. Some efforts are aimed specifically at women and minority graduate students to help prepare them for fields where they will be underrepresented. Other national efforts aim at rethinking graduate education. A conference in spring 2000 focused on revisioning the Ph.D. A national research project is currently examining innovative ways to reconceptualize the graduate education process to better prepare faculty for the new environment where teaching is paramount, applied research is more prevalent, technology and distance education are growing, and community service is a core commitment. Even though all these changes are under way, many programs, departments, and institutions understand little about the current graduate educational process, let alone the new set of challenges.

One helpful resource to better understand the forces that impact the lives of graduate students is *Socialization of Graduate and Professional Students in*

Higher Education: A Perilous Passage? The primary author, John C. Weidman, University of Pittsburgh, has spent his entire faculty career devoted to researching the lives of graduate students, helping us to better understand this part of the educational process that has received little attention. His coauthors, Darla J. Twale and Elizabeth L. Stein, offer insight into graduate education that is necessary for the successful development of any program or department.

The monograph begins with an examination of the socialization process, exploring stages of socialization, informal and formal socialization experiences, professional standards, student peer culture, the impact of key individuals on socialization, and ways to invest and involve new professionals through structured forms of engagement. For example, more experienced students can serve as guides for new students, and first year socialization courses provide a structured introduction into graduate study. Disciplinary differences are highlighted, for various fields have different cultures, professional standards, and organizational structures. The authors develop a framework for the socialization of graduate students that departments and programs should use to evaluate and assess their own efforts at socialization. In an era of assessment, this model will surely be a much used resource. The model is examined in light of the many current challenges in graduate education, including the growing diversity of students, technology, distance education, and modification of the faculty role. The authors also review other ongoing challenges, such as the need for greater enforcement of professional standards, concern about ethics, and support for students. This monograph will surely become the definitive resource on the socialization and education of graduate students.

Several other ASHE-ERIC Higher Education Reports will be of interest to readers. *Faculty Socialization as a Cultural Process* reviews the forces that affect socialization among new faculty. *Successful Faculty Development and Evaluation* suggests ways to socialize new faculty, specifically through faculty evaluation. One of the challenges noted in this monograph is the challenge women and people of color face in graduate school, which is examined among new faculty in *Faculty Job Satisfaction: Women and Minorities in Peril*. And *Empowering the Faculty: Mentoring Redirected and Renewed* examines one way to alleviate the many challenges faced by new faculty through the development of mentoring programs. I hope you find this ASHE-ERIC report valuable as you attempt to understand the current challenges of graduate education and socialization.

Adrianna J. Kezar
Series Editor
Director, ERIC Clearinghouse on Higher Education
Assistant Professor, The George Washington University

Acknowledgments

This manuscript would never have been written without the encouragement and patience of Jon Fife, editor of the ASHE-ERIC Higher Education Report series when the proposal for it was originally accepted. The current editor, Adrianna Kezar, has continued to be very supportive of our efforts. The authors are indebted to Ken Feldman for his careful reading, critique, and editorial suggestions for improving the manuscript. Jim Antony, Jeff Milem, Maresi Nerad, Bill Tierney, Vincent Tinto, and an anonymous reviewer also provided helpful comments. Graduate students in a seminar at the University of Dayton provided useful insights. In the end, however, the contents, warts and all, remain the authors' responsibility.

The Professions and Socialization

NEARLY TWENTY-FIVE YEARS AGO, Bragg (1976) published a monograph on the socialization of graduate and professional students in what was to become the ASHE-ERIC Higher Education Report series. This report stood as one of the most comprehensive treatments of this topic until Tierney and Rhoads (1994) published an ASHE-ERIC Higher Education Report on faculty socialization that included much of the same classic literature but used a cultural approach. While this work necessarily included the graduate experience as a component of anticipatory socialization into the higher education faculty role, Tierney and Rhoads (1994) did not concentrate on the socialization of graduate and professional students. Hence, it is appropriate at this time to expand, extend, and update the discourse on socialization in higher education.

Our primary goal is to build a conceptual framework for understanding the socialization of graduate and professional students that draws from the work of Tierney and Rhoads (1994) and Bragg (1976) as well as from research on adult socialization (Arnett, 2000; Mortimer and Simmons, 1978; Thornton and Nardi, 1975; Miller and Wagner, 1971) and the conceptual analyses of students' socialization in higher education at both the undergraduate (Weidman, 1989a, 1989b) and graduate levels (Stein and Weidman, 1989, 1990; Ondrack, 1975; Antony, forthcoming). Because the normative dimension of graduate education (including the development of values, ethics, and personal commitments to an identifiable group of professional colleagues) has been neglected by several of these authors, we frame our discussion in the broader context of graduate and professional student socialization. We take explicitly into consideration *both* substantive and normative dimensions of graduate education.

With the continuing desire of state legislatures, licensing bodies, and the public clientele of professionals to ensure the preparation of well qualified practitioners, such an analysis is particularly timely. In addition, our analysis reflects a further effort to order and provide conceptual underpinnings for issues raised in the current literature, including drawing implications for the redesign of postbaccalaureate programs engaged in professional preparation.

Despite the fact there are similarities among them, no two graduate and professional programs are identical, and no two students experience graduate or professional school in quite the same way. For instance, humanities and social science graduate students are held to expectations different from students in the natural sciences. Programs that prepare students for careers in academe differ from professional programs that prepare students for nonacademic careers. Master's and professional degree programs are different from doctoral degree programs. There are as many differences in content and approach across advanced academic and professional fields as there are within specific fields. Consequently, it is important to recognize that graduate students experience socialization processes that reflect their chosen fields and disciplines as well as their institutional homes.

No two graduate and professional programs are identical, and no two students experience graduate or professional school in quite the same way.

If entering graduate students are to succeed in their new environments, they must learn not only to cope with the academic demands but also to recognize values, attitudes, and subtle nuances reflected by faculty and peers in their academic programs. The importance of academic disciplines for undergraduate career development has been demonstrated convincingly in the empirical work of Smart, Feldman, and Ethington (2000). Antony (forthcoming) has used Smart, Feldman, and Ethington (2000) and the conceptual work of Weidman (1989a) and Stein and Weidman (1989, 1990) as a basis for arguing that similar processes of faculty and peer influence on students' professional career development occur at the graduate academic program level. Students learn to recognize normative expectations as well as the politics and pecking order among members of their programs as they prepare for futures in a graduate or professional field. To succeed, students must develop the capacity to observe who commands power and authority, who is rewarded and how, who is banished and why, which groups or individuals are treated fairly, and who is tokenized (Staton and Darling, 1989). They also need to be aware of the challenges that participation in a new culture presents to novices (Sheehy, 1977), including academic, personal, and financial demands. Our goal in preparing the present monograph is to provide insight into and a conceptualization of the sometimes perilous passage of students through advanced degree programs.

The Professions in Society

Our foremost concern is with the process of preparation for those occupations in which practitioners may be considered to be professionals, according to the following criteria:

1. *The professional practices a full-time* occupation, *which comprises the principal source of his earned income. . . .*
2. *The professional must be committed to a* calling, *that is the treatment of the* occupation, *and all of its requirements, as an enduring set of normative and behavioral expectations.*
3. *The professional is set apart from the laity by various signs and symbols, but by the same token is identified with his peers—often in formalized* organizations.
4. *The professional possesses esoteric, but useful knowledge and skills, based on specialized training or* education *of exceptional duration and perhaps of exceptional difficulty. . . .*
5. *The professional practices his occupation by perceiving the needs of individual or collective clients that are relevant to his competence and by attending to those needs by competent performance. . . .*
6. *The professional proceeds by his own judgment and authority; he thus enjoys* autonomy *restrained by responsibility* [Moore and Rosenbloom, 1970, pp. 5–6].

These criteria reflect the continuing expectation that professionals will be prepared at an advanced educational level to assume responsibility for practice of a career that is characterized by a high level of autonomy within the scope of the particular intellectual expertise defining the career. These characteristics include expectations about professional practice that are both normative (being committed to a calling and having a service orientation) and substantive (having an education of exceptional duration and difficulty). By this definition, one could argue that doctoral programs leading to academic careers in arts and sciences disciplines constitute professional preparation.

Consequently, we feel it is appropriate to focus on a range of postbaccalaureate preparation programs in higher education, including doctoral programs in arts and sciences disciplines as well as programs in traditional professional areas of study that were prominent in the earliest universities, namely, law, medicine, and theology. We also consider master's and doctoral level professional preparation in areas such as business, dentistry, education, public and educational administration, engineering, social work, architecture, library science, and nursing. In developing our conceptualization, we sought common themes across areas but also recognized the importance of considering how advanced degree programs differ by field and are experienced differently by students.

Characterizing Socialization

Following Brim (1966), we define the word *socialization* in a broad sense as "the process by which persons acquire the knowledge, skills, and dispositions that make them more or less effective members of their society" (p. 3). This definition is consistent with the classic study of medical students by Merton, Reader, and Kendall (1957) in which the authors assert that medical students "learn a professional role by so combining its component knowledge and skills, attitudes, and values as to be motivated and able to perform this role in a professionally and socially acceptable fashion" (p. 41). Because socialization contains cognitive as well as affective dimensions, to understand socialization into the professional areas we need to address both curricular (knowledge and skills) and normative (dispositions) aspects of graduate and professional students' experiences in higher education. We also need to understand the processes through which individual students are socialized into their chosen professional fields. The dispositional aspect is reflected especially in the development of commitments to and identification with a particular profession, including its ethical practice.

Socialization can also be characterized metaphorically. It can be thought of as "a train leaving the station" for a particular destination, that is, from matriculation to licensure. It becomes a continuum of experiences, with some experiences being commonly and uniformly felt by students and others perceived differently by students with different characteristics. Each step along the journey has particular significance, becomes a key rite of passage, or adds important people and information to the mix.

For the most part, in the socialization process graduate students must acquire new information through communication strategies that move them from stability to insecurity and uncertainty and then back to stability again as they maneuver in their new environments (Cahn, 1986; Staton, 1990). Socialization can be viewed as "an upward-moving spiral" carrying the neophyte through recurring processes toward the goal of professionalization. Those experiences may be repetitive, but each takes the student to a higher level of personal and professional maturity. Thus, each program follows a serial pattern (entry, advancement, exit) as the student passes through the formal and informal processes (Coombs, 1978), emerging more accomplished than at entry, changed in specific ways, and prepared to assume new professional roles. Again metaphorically, just as bullfrogs and butterflies undergo physical transformation during their life cycle, graduate students must also experience their own particular kind of metamorphosis to move into their postgraduate careers.

For the newcomer, socialization into a graduate degree program illuminates and modifies any romanticized versions of an unrealistically portrayed profession. In other words, "with each passage some magic must be given up, some cherished illusion of safety and comfortable, familiar sense of self must be cast off, to allow for the greater expansion of our own distinctiveness" (Sheehy, 1977, p. 21). Thus, socialization can take on a Pygmalion-like character like Eliza Doolittle in *My Fair Lady.*

Some believe socialization follows a dialectical pattern as students raise themselves to a higher level of cognitive and affective development (Staton, 1990). Thus, assuming new roles and learning to cope combine with what incumbents bring to their roles. More important, a transformation from outsider to insider takes place (Bullis and Bach, 1989). Events occurring early in a graduate or professional program differ from those near its conclusion, because they increase in difficulty and may change setting (for example, from classroom to clinic) as the student moves closer to the cherished goal. These events become turning points or key change factors that constitute the dialectic (Bragg, 1976; Staton, 1990).

Socialization has also been recognized as a subconscious process whereby persons internalize behavioral norms and standards and form a sense of identity and commitment to a professional field. Graduate and professional socialization necessitates shared conscious experiences and links with fellow students, faculty mentors, and role models as well as subject mastery and knowledge application (Ketefian, 1993). According to Stark (1998), "faculty in the preparation programs teach academic content, necessary professional skills, and the context of the profession, thus preparing the graduate to enter practice at a basic competency level" (p. 355). At the culmination of the socialization process, students should be able to answer three key questions: (1) What do I do with the skills I have learned? (2) What am I supposed to look like and act like in my professional field? and (3) What do I as a professional look like to other professionals as I perform my new roles? (Daresh and Playko, 1995).

Dimensions of Socialization

Tierney and Rhoads (1994, pp. 26–30) and Mario (1997, pp. 10–13) maintain that graduate and professional fields and disciplines in higher education exhibit the six polar dimensions of organizational socialization described by Van Maanen and Schein (1979): collective versus individual, formal versus informal, random versus sequential, fixed versus variable pace, serial versus disjunctive, and investiture versus divestiture. The following example illustrates how each of these dimensions is reflected in the socialization of graduate and professional students.

Collective socialization refers to the common set of experiences encountered by all graduate students in an academic program. *Individual socialization* refers to the processes experienced in "an isolated and singular manner" (Tierney and Rhoads, 1994, p. 27). With respect to the collective versus individual dimension in a medical school clinical setting, students maintain a collective identity as they are herded (and hounded) through rounds with experienced physicians. Conversely, all-but-dissertation (ABD) students in the arts and sciences generally have a more individualistic experience with their major professor.

Formal socialization refers to experiences designed specifically for accomplishing particular goals. *Informal socialization* refers to relatively unstructured experiences that are processed in various ways, depending on individual students. With respect to formal versus informal aspects, all schools offer formal rites of passage that track students through the program. Students, however, also learn the more informal departmental and peer cultures that, in turn, help them survive the formal structure.

Random socialization refers to "a progression of unclear or ambiguous steps," while *sequential socialization* refers to "discrete and identifiable steps for achieving an organizational role" (Tierney and Rhoads, 1994, p. 28). With respect to randomness of passage, some information supplied to novices is random, ambiguous, and subject to change (including opinions on courses and faculty). More formalized, detailed, and sequential information involves specific steps students must follow, such as required examinations or dissertation guidelines for acceptable documents.

Fixed pace refers to clearly defined, unchanging time frames within which progression must occur for all graduate students. *Variable pace* refers to vague and unclear time frames for significant milestones. With respect to pace of passage, time to completion of a graduate program leading to the doctorate is variable and depends on student and faculty pace as well as the nature of the research. By contrast, medical, law, dental, and M.B.A. students follow a more fixed, prescribed curriculum and time table.

Serial socialization refers to the existence of planned organizational structures and educational experiences through which novices are trained by faculty. According to Wheeler (1966, p. 60), "the recruit has been preceded by others who have been through the same process and who can teach him about the setting." In *disjunctive socialization,* "recruits are not following in the footsteps of predecessors" (p. 61). Tierney and Rhoades (1994, p. 29) suggest that disjunctive socialization in higher education occurs where "no role models are available for the organizational newcomer." This situation might occur in the case of new or significantly reformulated graduate programs, or when students with very different characteristics from their predecessors are enrolled.

With respect to consistency of passage, successful progression through the graduate or professional program often depends on whether one has a faculty mentor who is more than just an academic adviser: "Mentoring is a personal as well as professional relationship. An adviser might or might not be a mentor, depending on the quality of the relationship. A mentoring relationship develops over an extended period, during which a student's needs and the nature of the relationship tend to change. A mentor will try to be aware of these changes and vary the degree and type of attention, help, advice, information, and encouragement that he or she provides" (Committee on Science, Engineering, and Public Policy, 1997, p. 1). Those graduate students who also have previous knowledge of the role through anticipatory socialization experience serial socialization; those lacking this assistance and support that is often critical to success experience disjunctive socialization.

Finally, Tierney and Rhoads (1994) characterized *investiture* and *divestiture* as follows: "Investiture (more affirming) concerns the welcoming of the recruit's anticipatory socialization experiences and individual characteristics, whereas divestiture (more transforming) involves stripping away those personal characteristics seen as incompatible with the organizational ethos" (p. 29). The socialization process ultimately requires investiture for the student's transformation into the new professional role to be completed with an internalization of appropriate values, attitudes, and beliefs associated with their intended professions and professionalism. Confirmation of these values in the professional setting constitutes investiture in the student's chosen profession.

When there is a disjunctive situation in which new students are not accepted by faculty because they are not like their predecessors (females in predominantly male fields, students of color, nontraditional students), pressures toward divestiture of orientations perceived to be undesirable may be very strong. It may also be accompanied by divestiture after graduation in which novices are resocialized in profession-specific normative patterns, thereby creating dissonance among the socialization process, the expectations of graduate or professional training, and the stark realities inherent in the first job.

While the taxonomic work of Stark, Lowther, Hagerty, and Orczyk (1986) concentrates on the academic goals of professional education, it does not deal specifically with socialization. In a recent article, however, Stark (1998) addresses socialization directly in terms of something consciously and unconsciously woven into the preparation phase. For instance, the fields of nursing and social work "consciously socialize students to prepare them for client interaction" (p. 371). Professional socialization and identity formation for educators occur primarily during internships and field experiences. Engineering faculty socialize their students for systematic problem solving, while architects are socialized to see environmental sensitivity of man-made construction. Stark (1998) classifies the artistic disciplines as socializing for "self-discipline and dedication to the field" (p. 378). The affective processes through which master's, doctoral, and professional students confront those academic goals must also be understood to absorb the complexity of graduate and professional education.

Changes in higher education institutions, often necessitated through increasing pressures from external constituents, challenge long-standing academic goals. Bean (1998) observes that the language of the university has been moving more toward "efficiency, productivity, technology, . . . accountability, assessment, . . . total quality management" and away from "scholarship or learning community" (p. 497). While our examination of literature on professional and doctoral programs from the 1950s through the 1990s suggests that patterns of socialization continue to follow many of the long-standing norms associated with collegial culture, socialization processes are increasingly less homogeneous in much more diverse student populations. Taking these and other considerations into account, we describe in detail the socialization process for graduate and professional students in the next section.

Conceptualizing Socialization in Graduate and Professional Programs

THIS SECTION TAKES the framework for role acquisition developed by Thornton and Nardi (1975) and applies it to the socialization of graduate and professional students. This conceptualization is particularly appropriate for addressing socialization in graduate programs because it recognizes explicitly the developmental nature of the socialization process.

Stages of Socialization

Two characteristics of socialization are particularly salient for understanding the dynamics of graduate and professional programs: (1) that socialization is a developmental process, and (2) that certain core elements (knowledge acquisition, investment, and involvement) are linked to the development of role identity and commitment (Stein, 1992; Thornton and Nardi, 1975). Further, knowledge acquisition, investment, and involvement, which lead to role identity and commitment, can also be linked to the stages of role acquisition.

Thornton and Nardi (1975) used the word *stage* when they characterized role acquisition as a developmental process based on serial passage through a sequence of levels, each reflecting more intense role commitment. Of course, identity with and commitment to a professional role are not accomplished completely during professional preparation but rather continue to evolve after novices begin professional practice. Hence, as applied to the present view of professional socialization, *stages* reflect somewhat different states of identity and commitment that are overlapping rather than mutually exclusive.

Anticipatory Stage

In the anticipatory stage of role acquisition, an individual becomes aware of the behavioral, attitudinal, and cognitive expectations held for a role incumbent. This stage covers the preparatory and recruitment phases as the student enters graduate and professional programs with stereotypes and preconceived expectations. Sheehy (1977) refers to it as the *merger self.* Even though graduate students enter professional training programs with preconceived ideas about their chosen fields, they usually modify these views based on a clearer understanding of what they need to know and be able to do to be successful. Senge (1990) suggests that this process is difficult but necessary. During this stage, neophytes must also make a commitment to their quest and to their chosen professions (Bucher and Stellings, 1977).

One key source of information about the anticipated role is the mass media (for example, news stories, published articles, and so on). But information is also gleaned through the novice's personal observation of and interaction with current role incumbents, as well as through the novice's observation of the others who interact with, express attitudes about, or ascribe status to current role incumbents. Role information is generalized and stereotypical. Knowledge of anticipated roles gained through media and prospective role models helps to socialize only to the extent that it provides an accurate representation of the role (Stein, 1992).

Novices learn new roles, procedures, and agendas that must be followed. They exude uncertainty in terms of professional jargon, vocabulary, knowledge of subject content, normative behaviors, and acceptable emotions. Communication tends to be a one-way downward flow from professor, supervisor, and/or clinician to student. Novices generally seek information, listen carefully, and comply readily to faculty-initiated communication such as verbal imperatives and explicit directions for program success and eventual completion (Staton, 1990).

Formal Stage

During the formal stage of role acquisition, role expectations held by the novice remain idealized. Students are inducted into the program and determine their degree of fitness (Clark and Corcoran, 1986). This stage differs from the previous one, however, in that the novice receives formal instruction in the knowledge upon which future professional authority will be based. As an apprentice, the novice also observes the activities of role incumbents and older students and is able to learn about normative role expectations and how they are carried out, opportunities that are not generally available to the public. At this stage, there is general consensus among the primary agents of socialization (for example, faculty), current role incumbents, and students about the normative expectations that tend to be clearly stated and documented. Students are inducted into the program, practice role rehearsal, and thereby determine their degree of fitness, observe and imitate expectations through role taking, and become familiar faces in the program (Stein, 1992).

Novices eventually become veteran newcomers who have some seasoning but who still need concrete information on normative standards, rewards, and sanctions. Students interpret their environment, establish their professional goals, and seek positive feedback and modification in their continued growth and development (Clark and Corcoran, 1986; Staton and Darling, 1989). They are given and accept increasingly greater responsibility and privileges commensurate with past performance and increased maturity.

Communication becomes *informative* through learning course material, *regulative* through embracing normative expectations, and *integrative* through faculty and student interaction. Concern centers around task issues such as the difficulty and success of mastering academics as well as maneuvering successfully through the university environment. This stage also validates students as they complete successfully formal examinations and signals their passage toward program completion and professional goals (Staton, 1990). The quality of the program and concomitant experiences affect the thoroughness and success of the total socialization process. In other words, preparation is a function of the type and range of activities in which incumbents participate, how clearly standards and expectations of them are stated, and the time that is allotted for role-playing opportunities (Bucher and Stellings, 1977). To be successful, however, incumbents cannot remain in the formal stage but must also venture into and become charter members of the informal realm.

Informal Stage

During the informal stage of role acquisition, the novice learns of the informal role expectations. These "expectations arise and are transmitted by interactions with others" who are current role incumbents (Thornton and Nardi, 1975, p. 878). Through adept communication and immersion in the new culture, students receive behavioral clues, observe acceptable behavior, and, it is hoped, respond and react accordingly. While some of this information comes from faculty, students tend to develop their own peer culture and social and emotional support system among classmates (Staton and Darling, 1989).

As students pass through stages together in their quest for support and reassurance, they communicate their anxieties before passage and express their relief after securing passage to the next level. In some graduate programs, close-knit cohort groupings of student peers facilitate communication and support. They ease the social anxiety associated with fitting in and assign status to individual members. The socialization process varies as some students are ascribed ingroup status while others are less able to acclimate. Student cohorts develop as a community having a social and emotional identification, cohesiveness, and connectedness (Twale and Kochan, 2000).

The novice becomes aware of flexibilities in carrying out roles while still meeting role requirements. Less agreement exists about these flexible role expectations, and they "tend to be implicit and refer to the attitudinal and cognitive features of role performance" (Thornton and Nardi, 1975, p. 879). During the process, the student begins the transformation of feeling less student-like and more professional (Rosen and Bates, 1967). Formal classroom instruction, however, does not make the student a professional; the process needs closure from the academic realm as the novice reaches a professional level.

Personal Stage

In the personal stage of socialization, "individuals and social roles, personalities and social structures become fused" (Thornton and Nardi, 1975, p. 880), and the role is internalized. Students form a professional identity and reconcile the dysfunction and incongruity between their previous self-image and their new professional image as they assume their new role. They accept a value orientation, relinquish former ways, and resolve any conflict impeding a total role transformation (Bullis and Bach, 1989; Gottlieb, 1961). They separate themselves from the department in search of their own identity or what Sheehy (1977) calls the "seeker self." Through the process, however, graduate and professional students are to realize that their program is only preparatory to their professional goal, not the real thing (Olmstead and Paget, 1969).

The incumbents often need to "modify their self-conceptions by role-taking, observation, and participation" (Pease, 1967, p. 63). As students become deeply immersed in their program, they mature and experience compliance with values and attitudes, higher expectations of themselves as well as from the faculty, and more freedom; they eventually evolve into the ultimate role as scholar and colleague (Staton, 1990). Students can also seek formal recognition and status through securing assistantships, coveted fellowships, and scholarships (Staton, 1990; Twale and Kochan, 1998). During this critical synthesis, students focus on research interests, specialty areas, and becoming more involved with professional matters such as publication, presentation, and service (Brown and Krager, 1985).

The incumbent has learned how to accommodate the required normative dimensions of a role with his or her personal needs, attitudes, and occupational role requirements. At this point, students assess their career marketability, degree of competitiveness and aggressiveness needed to succeed in the professional world, scholarly concerns such as advancing knowledge in the field, and commitment to both personal and professional development beyond graduation (Stark, Lowther, and Hagerty, 1986).

Core Elements of Socialization

There has been considerable discussion in the literature of the process that leads to role acquisition. Some research has given primary importance to the transmission of normative role dimensions to students as a means of socializing (for example, Bragg, 1976; Merton, Reader, and Kendall, 1957) and has analyzed socialization at the institutional level. Others deny that knowledge of the normative role dimensions yields commitment (for example, Becker and Carper, 1956a, 1956b) and have placed primary emphasis on the individual level of analysis of the socialization process. For the present discussion, knowledge acquisition, investment, and involvement are presumed to be the core elements that lead to identification with and commitment to a professional role (Stein, 1992; Thornton and Nardi, 1975).

Knowledge Acquisition

Knowledge acquisition is relevant to socialization in two ways. First, novices must acquire sufficient cognitive knowledge and skills for effective professional role performance. Second, novices must acquire affective knowledge such as awareness of normative expectations associated with the professional role being sought, a realistic assessment of personal ability to perform the demands of professional roles successfully, and awareness of the confidence others have in the novice's capacity to practice professional roles successfully (Stein, 1992).

During socialization, knowledge shifts from being general to being specialized and complex. The novice begins to understand the problems and ideology characteristic of the chosen profession and to understand why alternative professions were rejected. The novice becomes aware of his or her capacity to participate in a professional culture because he or she knows its language, heritage, and etiquette. The novice begins to act and feel like an incumbent, which leads to identification with the role (Becker and Carper, 1956a, 1956b; Sherlock and Morris, 1967). In all stages, the accuracy of knowledge and of the novice's personal assessment of capacity to perform the professional role successfully will influence socialization outcomes.

One of the most important outcomes of professional socialization is an evolving professional identity.

One of the most important outcomes of professional socialization is an evolving professional identity. Social identity theory posits that, beginning in the preprofessional stages and continuing through graduation, students cloak themselves in a professional identity, which usually forces a modification of their personal identity such that the two are intertwined and compatible rather than dissonant and competing (Ronkowski and Iannaccone, 1989).

Investment

A second core element associated with the development of role identity and commitment is investment. To invest in a role is to commit something of personal value such as time, alternative career choices, self-esteem, social status, or reputation to some aspect of a professional role or preparation for it. During the anticipatory stage of socialization, the novice applies to and enrolls in a particular school. In doing so, the possibility of attending another educational institution or pursing an alternative career is rejected or at least temporarily postponed. As the novice begins to develop a commitment to a particular professional role and its related status, contemplating a change in educational institutions or professional aspirations becomes increasingly difficult (Geer, 1966).

During the formal stage of socialization, the novice enrolls in classes that provide specialized knowledge. This investment in learning specialized material and skills that are not usually transferable to other occupations can be considerable in terms of time and money spent. During the informal and personal stages of socialization, more specialized knowledge is acquired that creates an even greater investment (Stein, 1992).

Of great importance as well is the sponsorship of the novice by a role incumbent or professor that may occur at this stage. Sponsorship can create a sense of obligation to live up to the expectations of the sponsor and thus increase commitment to the role. Accepting sponsorships thus results in deeper commitments to the professional role (Sherlock and Morris, 1967, p. 38).

Just as the impact of knowledge acquisition is limited by the accuracy of the knowledge available, the impact of the process of investment is limited by the value placed on the investment action by the novice. For instance, a novice who has limited concern for extending the time spent in career preparation will feel less committed to the original course of action than one who, for whatever reason, feels obliged to complete educational preparation as expediently as possible (Stein, 1992).

Professional socialization depends to a great extent on the neophyte student's goals, level of commitment to those goals, commitment to the program and discipline being studied, level of investment given to the program in terms of money, time, and psychic energy, and personal pride in previous accomplishments and future expectations. Investment emphasizes sponsorship by faculty and the transmission of more accepted values of the discipline or profession that are germane to successful professional practice (Breneman, 1975; Slawski, 1973).

Involvement

A third core element associated with the development of role identity and commitment is involvement. Involvement is participation in some aspect of the professional role or in preparation for it. Involvement theory has specific implications for graduate and student socialization in terms of how extensively students immerse themselves in their program. Levels of intensity vary as students progress through their program and as rites of passage (exams, licensure) necessitate their undivided attention (Astin, 1984; Brown, 1970). Social participation is the action by which novices acquire and internalize an occupational identity, develop an interest in a profession's problems, and take pride in perfecting technical skills (Becker and Carper, 1956a, p. 289).

Involvement with teachers and older students gives the novice insights into professional ideology, motives, and attitudes. Becker, Geer, Hughes, and Strauss (1961, p. 19) suggest "that human behavior is to be understood as a process in which the person shapes and controls his conduct by taking into account (through the mechanism of 'role taking') the expectations of others with whom he interacts." The process of role taking can thus be construed as a central element in the development of the professional self-image. Finally, it is involvement in the role and thinking about the personal meaning of participation in that role that brings about professional role identification (Oleson and Whittaker, 1968). To explain socialization using the theory of symbolic interaction, graduate and professional students do not passively respond to specific situations; rather, they actively extract clues to their behavior and continually evaluate themselves in the context of peers, faculty mentors, program expectations, and personal goals. Although students may resemble their mentors, they have the power and potential to modify the standard socialization process as they evaluate their progression through it. As a result, each incumbent reflects upon his or her own common as well as specific experiences. Some professions lend themselves more clearly to uniformity of process and outcome, while other graduate programs celebrate the uniqueness of each student's contribution to the discipline (Ronkowski and Iannaccone, 1989).

Although an effort has been made thus far to discuss each core element individually, the elements are clearly interrelated. For example, it is acquisition of specialized knowledge and skills (knowledge acquisition) coupled with participation in formal preparation for a professional role (investment) that promotes identification with and commitment to a professional role. Similarly, it is the student's interaction with role incumbents (involvement) that provides opportunities to become aware of appropriate professional attitudes (knowledge) and to be sponsored for membership in a profession (an investment) (Stein, 1992).

> **Although students may resemble their mentors, they have the power and potential to modify the standard socialization process as they evaluate their progression through it.**

Structural Engagement

For individual students, the development of a professional role identity and commitment are outcomes of socialization that reflect structural engagement. Kanter (1968) claims that there are three types of commitment: cognitive, cohesion, and control. *Cognitive commitment* refers to identification with the problems, tasks, and knowledge associated with professional roles. Cognitive commitment begins early in the socialization process as the result of the novice's investment of time and effort in acquiring specific knowledge, as well as his or her investment in the status of the role and pride in ability to carry out expected role functions adequately.

Cohesion commitment results from a novice's relationships with others—for example, through sponsorship of a novice by an adviser or affective ties within the student cohort or the professional community. Sponsorship develops commitment because of the novice's sense of obligation to live up to the standards of the sponsor. Similarly, individuals claiming to be members of a community willingly adopt normative role expectations out of a sense of commitment and loyalty to the group. Commitment is also engendered through interpersonal relationships among faculty and graduate students, including shared socioemotional goals for students' education (Slawski, 1973).

The third type is *control commitment*. Although this type of commitment has been associated with religious communities, it also has relevance for socialization into professional roles because it refers to the development of "values and inner convictions [that] morally obligate" the novice to a course of action (Kanter, 1968, p. 501). Through socialization, the novice internalizes the problems, ideology, and motives of a professional role, merges them with personal role expectations, and develops an obligation to carry out role expectations. The quality of interaction and the intensity of relationships among graduate students, faculty, and professional practitioners socialize students toward professional expectations (Miller, 1966).

Assumption of a full-fledged professional identity is not just an endpoint but should also reflect commitment to a continuous socialization process over the life course during which there is periodic modification of attitudes, perceptions, and role behavior. This is purposive socialization and a conscious choice for the incumbent, not a voluntary acceptance associated with the natural growth process. In fact, neophytes must establish a pattern of sublimating and modifying existing self-concepts to be able to maintain a high level of performance in chosen professional roles.

That acclimation to a subordinate student role is generally necessary for successful progression to professional status also reflects a type of resocialization. Depending on students' personalities and stage of personal development, they may vary considerably in the ability to incorporate these new subordinate roles and statuses into their lives. In addition, resocialization may require students to abandon previous roles and values and adopt the values, attitudes, beliefs, and identity of a new professional that, in certain instances, conflicts with one's preexisting character (Egan, 1989; Miller, 1966). In some instances, faculty select a very homogeneous student body to maximize the intensity of socialization processes and the uniformity of graduates.

Role identity and commitment are claimed to be a means of promoting professional social order (for example, Becker and Carper, 1956a, 1956b; Geer, 1966). It is argued that the normative dimensions of a professional role are especially important in socialization, because it is to the normative dimensions of a professional role that a prospective role incumbent initially identifies and commits. Further, the normative role dimensions are an important part of the core elements in the socialization process (i.e., knowledge acquisition, investment, and involvement).

Table 1 represents a structural-functional approach to describing the relationships among the stages of socialization, core socialization elements, and fundamental outcomes of professional socialization (for example, the development of role identity and commitment in novices) occurring through the student's engagement in the organizational structure of a graduate degree program. Listed vertically on the left are the four stages of role acquisition (anticipatory, formal, informal, and personal) identified by Thornton and Nardi (1975).

Three core socialization elements are listed in the center of Table 1: knowledge acquisition, investment, and involvement. On the right side of the chart are aspects of engagement in the structure of graduate programs reflecting various elements of identification with and commitment to professional roles at each stage of the socialization process.

Suggestions of how the socialization process might be evident at a given stage appear in the cells formed by the intersection of the four stages of socialization with the three core elements. Placement of comments in the cells is not meant to indicate a precise relationship between a given stage of socialization and either the core elements of socialization or the outcome of socialization. Rather, the comments are meant to suggest that, in general, movement is from the institution to the individual, from the general to the specific. In the next section, we develop an overarching conceptual framework for understanding the processes of socialization in graduate and professional programs.

TABLE 1
Core Elements and the Functional Approach to Professional Socialization

| Stages | Core Elements | | | Structural Engagement |
	Knowledge Acquisition	Investment	Involvement	Nature of Identity and Commitment
Anticipatory	Learns general role expectations through mass media and observation of role incumbents. Accuracy of knowledge a factor because of outsider status.	States interest in role and its status by applying to/enrolling in school and rejecting alternatives. Financial and temporal (full- versus part-time status) investment.	Admission and matriculation create sense of involvement in role. Becomes an "insider." Begins to think of self in role. May "shadow" a professional in the field.	Identification is with stereotypical dimensions of role. Disengages from conflicting roles, other possible professional roles.
Formal	Didactic instruction primary source of knowledge of argot, heritage, etiquette of role. Begins to achieve some competence in required knowledge and skills. Expectations of these dimensions are clear. Begins to understand why alternative roles/institutions were rejected. Sorting and selecting of students by faculty.	Specialized knowledge, educational policies, social value of consistency, pride and self-esteem make change difficult. Includes values, attitudes, ethics, and beliefs of the profession.	Interacting with others provides opportunity to compare own skill and competence in performing role and motives for choosing profession with role incumbents and other students. Reflects on own performance. Demonstrates competence in some role tasks. Sometimes treated as role incumbent. Rites of passage, exams passed, fellowships, internships.	Identifies with problems, ideology, motives, required normative dimensions or role. Seeks licensure/certification. Conducts research to advance a discipline, writes doctoral dissertation.

Informal	Learns informal (implicit) role expectations. Attains status within student or other informal group.	Tenure in role and sponsorship of incumbents and faculty make giving up role increasingly difficult. Claim of being in role forces novice to act as if it were true. Development of faculty-student bonds.	Increasing involvement with role incumbents leads to learning implicit role dimensions. Participation in role activities increases perception of competence. Mechanical solidarity with other students.	Increasing identification with personalized professional role. Interaction with professional practitioners.
Personal	Can perform cognitive dimensions of role with adequate skill and competence. Preparation for exams, oral defenses of work.	Sponsorship based on professional competence as well as manner in which role tasks are performed. Creates an increasing sense of obligation to live up to expectations. One-on-one mentoring.	Increasing sense of solidarity with role incumbents. Clinical experience; joint presentations and publication with faculty.	Professional and personal role needs generally congruent. Claims "to be" a professional. Secure job in profession, ethical practice.

Source: Stein, 1992, p. 27.

A Framework for the Socialization of Graduate and Professional Students

B ECAUSE THE MODEL of undergraduate socialization developed by Weidman (1989a) is one of the most recognized conceptual frameworks for socialization in higher education (reprinted in Pascarella and Terenzini, 1991; Chickering and Reisser, 1993; Bess and Webster, 1999), it is the foundation we use to address the socialization of graduate and professional students. We acknowledge that this model is fundamentally structural-functional and hence could well be revised to include a broader range of perspectives in its elaboration than in our previous work (Stein and Weidman, 1989, 1990).

For instance, Tierney (1997) criticizes the Weidman framework (1989a) by suggesting that it ignores the possibility of a socialization process that is more unique, individualistic, and reflective of the diverse nature of the more recent incumbents to academic and professional roles as well as the changing environments affecting them. The increasing numbers of graduate students of color as well as women entering professional and academic degree programs create challenges for professors who previously encountered a more homogeneous, predominantly white male clientele. The next subsections illustrate progressively more interactive approaches to socialization, starting with the traditional, linear notion of socialization in organizations.

Linear Models of Socialization

We refer to traditional models of socialization as the Standard Plan, represented by the linear diagram in Figure 1 (see O'Toole, 1996). The linear configuration depicts a process whereby program faculty admit students, socialize

FIGURE 1
Standard Plan

1	2	3
Admit the student based on standard criteria	Socialize the student	Graduate, license, or certify the student

them in some prescribed fashion, and graduate them after a specific program of study has been completed. Graduation may be followed by additional study and/or examinations for professional licensure or state certification. While linear programs do develop professionals, the processes underlying them lack a mechanism for feedback. Much like Demings's concept of total quality management, adapted for academe as continuous quality improvement, socialization and professionalization need not be linear. They can reflect changes in program expectations and desired outcomes (O'Toole, 1996). What is distinctive, then, is the concerted effort by existing faculty and professionals in a professional or disciplinary field to continually address the issue of whether graduates are prepared adequately to perform the roles for which they have been socialized so that the graduate program providing preparation can make appropriate adjustments. Desirable, but not always present, are regular opportunities for the voices of graduate students to be heard so that their perspectives inform program development.

Nonlinear Models of Socialization

A fundamental concern is whether the socialization process has been designed by faculty to support the student's current role as student or the student's future role as professional (Baird, 1990; Golde, 2000). More extensive interaction among participants and the introduction of greater student participation in normative dimensions of socialization has become increasingly more important as both structures of institutional governance and more heterogeneous populations of students have changed the academic context. Consequently, it is appropriate to characterize socialization according to the new plan illustrated in Figure 2 as a circular, seamless model encouraging feedback among all participants to enhance the process (see O'Toole, 1996).

FIGURE 2
New Plan

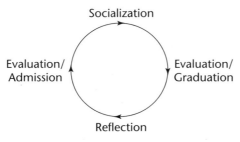

Internal University Community

Graduate and professional programs decide whom to admit based on faculty expectations, university standards, and desired professional outcomes. After admission, students are socialized into graduate study as well as for professional roles. Both faculty and practitioners should engage in a reflective process to determine whether students are ready to assume professional roles. Faculty should examine the academic program to determine whether it provides the student with the information necessary to perform professional roles. Students should evaluate their personal fitness for the new professional roles and determine what they may still need to perform them more effectively. This information should also feed back into the program and practical experiences so that what is being done can be assessed and necessary improvements made (see O'Toole, 1996).

Twale and Kochan (1999) present a dynamic and interactive model (as opposed to a linear model), one that merges student input and experiential knowledge with faculty contributions of theoretical, empirical, and analytical information in a program that revolves so it can also evolve. Twale and Kochan's development of a community of learners (1999) emphasizes personal, professional, and academic connectedness throughout a doctoral program that serves as a networking strategy before and even after graduation. They take the somewhat insular new plan in Figure 2 a step further to the collaborative plan shown in Figure 3, illustrating a more expansive circle that becomes interactive beyond the university confines and encourages the flow of information between the practical and academic world of students and faculty. Figures 2 and 3 imply

FIGURE 3
Collaborative Plan

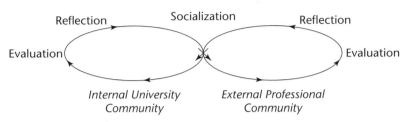

receptivity to a variety of both interpersonal and technological means for facilitating open communication and information flow, whether participants are on campus or at a distance.

The core elements of socialization (Table 1) may be construed as supporting a primarily linear approach to socialization similar to that reflected in Figure 1. Consequently, it is necessary to develop a revised version of the socialization process in terms of the ways in which contemporary graduate and professional student socialization reflects the seamless, interactive models shown in Figures 2 and 3. Table 2 is a modification of Table 1 that suggests such a revision. At the graduate level, anticipatory socialization includes more vivid images of academic and professional fields as well as of the graduate programs and universities in which they are housed. Less mystique surrounds the professional and access to him/her is promoted so that a more realistic self-assessment by the graduate student of her/his potential to fill anticipated professional roles is possible. Prospective students can more definitely evaluate any preconceived notions about the professions to which they are aspiring and dismiss outmoded mental models in favor of more accurate ones.

With a shift from a primarily teaching model at the undergraduate level to a much more interactive learning model at the graduate level (Barr and Tagg, 1995), formal socialization stands to change as well. Technology is woven into the curriculum, thereby necessitating changes in instructional delivery and faculty preparation. Course sequencing and cohort groupings evolve into learning communities, be they on campus or through distance learning (Shapiro and Levine, 1999). Students are involved in more group activities, team projects, and reflective practice, collaborating with a diverse group of faculty, peer

TABLE 2
Core Elements and the Collaborative Approach to Professional Socialization

| Stages | Core Elements | | | Collaborative Engagement |
	Knowledge Acquisition	Investment	Involvement	Nature of Identity and Commitment
Anticipatory	Simulations, Web sites, CD-ROMs, videos of institution or profession.	Matriculation, financial investment, tolerance of diversity, inclusiveness.	Shadowing professionals, preprofessional experiences, insider versus outsider, self-assessment.	Evaluate mental models of the profession, identify with the professional role.
Formal	Transformative projects, learning communities, incorporate technology in the curriculum, adaptive evaluation strategies, new instructional delivery methods, distance learning courses, new learning paradigms.	Team learning; clear, realistic guidelines.	Shared vision; cohort groups; experiential activities; collaborative communities of faculty, students, and practitioners; reflective journals; mastery learning.	Conference presentations, professional development, joint research projects, acceptance of ideologies, professional community of learners, mutual evaluations, professional collaboration, advancing the profession through research.
Informal	Studenthood role, academic interactions, role learning, cyber competence, cyber receptivity.	Mutual sharing, group maturity, embrace diversity in class, faculty/student bonding, sociocultural activity, social interactions, collaborative dialogue, study groups.	Collaborative communities of faculty, students, and practitioners; group cohesiveness.	Professional interaction, practitioner interaction, appreciate diverse colleagues, networking, role identification, self-reflection.
Personal	Listserv, Internet, chat rooms, bulletin boards, personal mastery, personal vision, faculty and students become familiar with new technologies that affect teaching and learning.	Formal mentoring, sponsorship.	Formal mentoring by faculty and practitioners, clerkships, field experiences, practica, internships, assistantships, role identification.	Internalize professional role, connectedness to professionals, independent thinking, self-evaluation, ethical practice, role transformation.

Source: Thornton & Nardi, 1975.

colleagues, and practitioners from the field. Eventually, student inquiry becomes validated and acknowledged through conference participation and journal publication. Students no longer depend just on faculty for evaluation but receive assessments from multiple sources, including self-evaluation.

Informal socialization always contains peer interaction as a core component, but the types of communication expand to include technology. Students engage in less competitive classroom formats and in more collaborative dialogue that embraces diverse populations and perspectives. Group cohesiveness through sociocultural activities is imperative if students are to practice networking and interpersonal skills.

The personal element is also enhanced by exposure to advanced knowledge in their graduate fields and the use of new technology as incumbents begin to learn more about themselves, their chosen professions, and each other. Experiences are enriched by carefully crafted internships and formal mentoring that help students to connect with their chosen professions as well as with practicing professionals. Graduate students internalize professional roles while also developing the capacity for the ethical practice of autonomous careers in their chosen fields.

An Interactive Framework for the Socialization of Graduate and Professional Students

The Weidman Undergraduate Socialization Framework

Weidman's framework for undergraduate socialization (1989a) incorporates literature on college impact, including student characteristics, environmental press, interpersonal processes, and impacts of formal and informal dimensions of higher education institutions. Weidman's framework (1989a) emphasizes the importance of considering both interaction among the academic and social normative contexts and the socialization processes themselves on the collegiate experience, focusing on three basic dimensions: intrapersonal, interpersonal, and integration. Interpersonal processes represent the frequency and intensity of the social interactions of the student with others in the academic setting. Intrapersonal processes represent a student's subjective assessment of the collegiate experience as well as formal and informal learning. Integration represents the student's perceived "fit or subjective assessment of his or her degree of social integration into the life of the institution" (Weidman, 1989a, p. 33).

The Stark, Lowther, Hagerty, and Orczyk Framework

Socialization in graduate and professional programs likewise encompasses cognitive and affective components that are consistent with Stark, Lowther, Hagerty, and Orczyk's profile (1986) of professional programs that includes external influences, internal organization, aspects of the curriculum, and expected outcomes. The traditional view of socialization frequently associated with professional education is that in which the socializing agent or agencies identify the normative dimensions of a professional role and convey them to the students through both informal (for example, role modeling) and formal (for example, didactic instruction, rewards, and sanctions) means (Pease, 1967). The novice learns appropriate role behavior through didactic instruction and though interaction with others who already hold the appropriate normative beliefs about society and appropriate professional role performance (Brim, 1966; Wheeler, 1966; Clausen, 1968) and who reward or punish the novice for congruent or incongruent behavior.

In this vein, the process of socialization "entails a continuing interaction between the individual and those who seek to influence him" (Clausen, 1968, p. 3) and can be expected to occur when normative role dimensions are transmitted to novices during planned educational experiences. The extent to which socialization is successful depends on such things as how clearly the normative role dimensions have been identified, the degree of consensus among socializers about those dimensions, the selection of effective means for transmitting the normative elements of the role to the novice, and the extent to which there is tension or discontinuity between old and new roles or between the individual needs of novices and expected role behavior (Bush and Simmons, 1981; Getzels, 1963; Merton, Reader, and Kendall, 1957; Mortimer and Simmons, 1978; Ondrack, 1975; Sherlock and Morris, 1967).

The Bragg Framework

A similar notion of professional socialization is presented by Bragg (1976), who describes it as a process that allows education to achieve its goals of transmitting the "knowledge and skills, the values and attitudes and habits and modes of thought of the society to which he [or she] belongs" (p. 1). She contends that because the "components of the socialization process can be identified, . . . the conditions for maximizing both cognitive and affective development can be built into the learning process" (p. 3). Students "learn a professional role by so combining its component knowledge and skills, attitudes and values as to be motivated and able to perform this role in a professionally and socially acceptable fashion" (Merton, Reader, and Kendall, 1957, p. 41).

Bragg (1976) assumes that the expected outcomes of education are known and widely accepted and that members of the student body in a professional program will respond similarly to the educational process. The process of socialization is thus assumed to be a linear, unidirectional relationship among the variables: the students, the socialization mechanisms, and the anticipated outcomes. This type of approach is reflected in Figure 1 and Table 1. For those who are able to accept these assumptions, an advantage of Bragg's perspective is that the socialization process will appear to be rationalized and outcomes explained relatively easily. Further, it is presumably possible to identify the desired impact of professional education and to select and implement a plan that research, experience, "common sense," or tradition suggests will bring about the results desired. It is assumed that the educational evaluation process is relatively simple because the efficiency and effectiveness of the socialization process in achieving its stated goals can be readily assessed (Stein, 1992).

If unintended outcomes diminish predictability, the findings can be attributed to the imperfect identification of variables rather than to a theoretical or analytic flaw. Researchers are encouraged to rectify the problem by defining more precisely the elements of the process (for example, Burrell and Morgan, 1979). For example Carroll (1971) and Ondrack (1975) claimed that students' characteristics or structural dimensions of the socializing institutions have an impact on socialization outcomes. Both Carroll (1971) and Ondrack (1975) challenged assumptions of students' homogeneity and emphasized the necessity of precisely defining the antecedent and independent variables so that research findings might adequately explain socialization outcomes.

Critics of Bragg (1976) claim that she ignores the effects of graduate students' perceptions (Wentworth, 1980) and gender on the ways in which individuals perform professional roles (Gilligan, 1978). Further, even those writing from a functional perspective would criticize her implicit linear approach as having limited capacity to account for change in normative role expectations over time (Thornton and Nardi, 1975). Others (for example, Feldman, 1974; Gilligan, 1978) charge that the assumptions of students' homogeneity and normative consensus required by perspectives like Bragg's limit women's opportunities for equal access to professional status.

Epstein (1970) argues that professions are characterized by shared norms and attitudes that are generally associated with males, while women are traditionally socialized to different levels and types of motivation not generally associated with professional behavior (p. 167). Further, because "women do not display the normative characteristics associated with anticipatory socialization they are not as readily admitted to professional schools, the admissions committees either believing that women lack prior socialization or because they assume a lack of commitment and drive on the part of the female" (p. 168). Feldman (1974) agrees that women are socialized to norms and values that are often viewed as incompatible with success in graduate school. He, too, attacks the practice of allowing norms and values associated with the male role to be viewed as inherently intrinsic components of the professional role toward which socialization is directed.

The Stein and Weidman Graduate Socialization Framework
The approach by Stein and Weidman (1989, 1990) is similar to Bragg's work (1976) in that it uses a fundamentally structural-functional perspective for explaining how higher education socializes graduate students to meet the required normative dimensions of social and occupational roles. The framework differs from Bragg (1976), however, in maintaining that socialization is a complex developmental process that can be analyzed at either the group or individual level. It describes the complexity of the socialization process by demonstrating the relationships among students' background characteristics, university experiences, socialization outcomes, and mediating elements such as personal and professional communities both before and during the graduate school experience (Stein, 1992).

Contrary to the linear relationship between socialization elements assumed by Bragg's model (1976), the elements in both the Weidman (1989a) and

Stein and Weidman (1989, 1990) frameworks are assumed to be linked in a bidirectional fashion. There is a reciprocity of influences on the student such that the context and processes of the educational experience influence each other and the socialization outcomes affect the normative context of the higher education environment experienced by students (Kerckhoff, 1976). Socialization is conceived as reflecting the interaction between and among the various constituent elements rather than being a strictly linear, causal phenomenon, and as illustrating that socialization is also a developmental process.

The Stein and Weidman (1989, 1990) framework for graduate student socialization was not concerned with cognitive outcomes per se but with knowledge acquisition as an important element of socialization. Professional education is clearly meant to prepare individuals for a set of social and intellectual roles, the performance of which reflects an advanced level of specialized knowledge and skills. Learning was, however, included as a significant process of socialization.

Both the Bragg (1976) and the Stein and Weidman (1989, 1990) frameworks draw upon research focusing on the socializing impact of normative contexts and interpersonal relations among an organization's members (Brim, 1966; Wheeler, 1966) and acknowledge the effects of normative consensus and clarity (Bucher and Stellings, 1977; Katz and Hartnett, 1976; Ondrack, 1975). Stein and Weidman (1989, 1990), however, show that competing socializing agents and the novice's personal needs or interpretation of the context may alter the socializing experience as well as its impact (Oleson and Whittaker, 1968).

Further, the Stein and Weidman (1989, 1990) framework suggests that the socialization process can be analyzed at both the institutional and individual levels (Getzels, 1963; Thornton and Nardi, 1975). At the institutional level, the framework suggests that novices are integrated into the professional community by adopting its required norms, attitudes, and values and, because of them, are granted access to the authority and status of professional roles (Thornton and Nardi, 1975). The Stein and Weidman (1989, 1990) framework, however, shows that role expectations or norms also evolve because of the impact of the novice in individually shaping more personal professional roles and because of the impact over time of professional groups and others in reformulating normative expectations for professional roles.

At each stage, "interaction [occurs] between individuals and external expectations, including the individuals' attempts to influence the expectations of others as well as others to influence individuals" (Thornton and Nardi, 1975, p. 873). Clearly then, "socialization is not merely the transfer from one group to another in a static social structure, but the active creation of a new identity through a personal definition of the situation" (Reinharz, 1979, p. 374). Socialization is "a product of a gradual accumulation of experiences of certain people, particularly those with whom we stand in primary relations, and significant others who are actually involved in the cultivation of abilities, values and outlook" (Manis and Meltzer, 1968, p. 168).

The tension between individual needs and institutional role requirements (Getzels, 1963) may change the way professional roles are interpreted and performed. Moreover, normative role expectations change because of reinterpretation of the role by novices and socializing agents and because of changing social requirements, the efforts of professional associations, and the impact of current professional practice. The socialization experience differs from person to person because of individual interpretation or construction of the meaning of an event in which the student is involved (Stein, 1992).

Following the conceptual lead of Thornton and Nardi (1975), Stein and Weidman (1989, 1990) suggest that socialization occurs in four stages: anticipatory, formal, informal, and personal. The notion of stages in a complex process is consistent with the work of Tinto (1993) on institutional departure, arguably the inevitable outcome of unsuccessful socialization. Implicit in the Stein and Weidman (1989, 1990) framework is the importance of culture in higher education, defined as "the collective, mutually shaping patterns of norms, values, practices, beliefs, and assumptions that guide the behavior of individuals and groups in an institute of higher education and provide a frame of reference within which to interpret the meaning of events and actions on and off campus" (Kuh and Whitt, 1988, p. 12). Institutional culture provides the climate for diverse groups of students (Hurtado, Milem, Clayton-Pedersen, and Allen, 1999), the structure for students' progression through their degree programs (for example, exams and "rites of passage"), and the symbols and ceremonies (for example, graduation, honors convocations) that signify their accomplishments (Kuh and Witt, 1988; Tierney and Rhoads, 1994; Tinto, 1993).

Socialization in graduate programs is a nonlinear process during which identity and role commitment are developed through experiences with formal and informal aspects of university culture as well as personal and professional reference groups outside academe. The impacts of the various elements of the socialization process and the anticipated outcomes vary and are constantly developing. The role toward which socialization is directed moves from being a normatively defined one to a conceptualization of the anticipated role that reflects both required social expectations and the personal requirements, abilities, and expectations that the individual brings to the socialization experience. The outcome of socialization is not the transfer of a social role, but identification with and commitment to a role that has been both normatively and individually defined.

> **The outcome of socialization is identification with and commitment to a role that has been both normatively and individually defined.**

In summary, the Stein and Weidman (1989, 1990) framework suggests that socialization into the professions may be conceived as a process whereby the novice (1) enters the graduate educational program with values, beliefs, and attitudes about self and anticipated professional practice; (2) is exposed to various socializing influences while pursuing a graduate degree, including normative pressures exerted by institutional culture through faculty and peers as well as by society, professional organizations, professional practice, and personal reference groups; (3) assesses the salience of the various normative pressures for attaining personal and professional goals; and (4) assumes, changes, or maintains those values, aspirations, identity, and personal commitments that were held at the onset of the socializing experience.

The Weidman, Twale, and Stein Graduate Socialization Framework

Figure 4 shows a further modification of the original Stein and Weidman (1989, 1990) framework for understanding the socialization of graduate and professional students that has been expanded for this monograph by incorporating the stages of socialization described by Thornton and Nardi (1975) as well as more flexible and interactive approaches to understanding social phenomena.

FIGURE 4
Conceptualizing Graduate and Professional Student Socialization

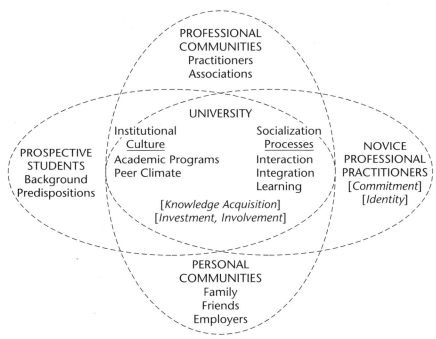

Interactive Stages of Socialization: Anticipatory, Formal, Informal, Personal

This expanded framework for understanding contemporary socialization processes of graduate and professional students takes into consideration differences as well as common threads and expectations among various types of students, academic and professional fields, and anticipated career outcomes. It illustrates the nonlinear, dynamic nature of professional socialization and the elements that promote identity with and commitment to professional roles. The framework in Figure 4 suggests that identification with and commitment to professional roles are complex, continuous, and developmental.

At the center of Figure 4 is the core socialization experience in the graduate degree program, consisting of the institutional culture (academic programs, peer climate) of the university, the socialization processes (interaction, integration, learning), and the core elements of socialization (knowledge acquisition, investment, involvement). This is the segment of the socialization process over which the academic program in the university has primary control. It is the academic program faculty who establish the norms for teaching, research, and service within the constraints of the larger university community. Faculty shape the curriculum as well as the organization of instruction and social relationships among members of the academic program. Faculty admit students and decide on the kinds of financial support to be offered.

Graduate students coming into the academic program experience its culture and are socialized into their chosen professional fields through learning, interaction with faculty and peers, and integration into its activities. During the course of their studies, graduate students acquire new knowledge, become involved in the life of their academic programs and career fields, experience the peer climate, and invest in developing the capacities necessary to become professional practitioners in their chosen areas. They also adapt to the institutional culture as it impinges on the passage to their degrees in both academic (exams and other requirements) and social (campus diversity) spheres.

Surrounding the central portion of Figure 4 are four other components of graduate student socialization: prospective students (background, predispositions), professional communities (practitioners, associations), personal communities (family, friends, employers), and novice professional practitioners. The components are arranged in concentric ellipses to represent the relationship among them as nonlinear and interactive. These components interact with the central elements of socialization during the course of the graduate educational experience and afterward as graduates move into the novice professional phase of their career development. While all of these elements exist to a significant extent outside the university setting, they have varying degrees of influence on academic programs and the graduate students enrolled in them.

The left side of Figure 4 includes the background (undergraduate education, ethnicity, race, gender, sexual orientation, for example) and predispositions (values, career aspirations, learning styles, beliefs, and so on) of students aspiring to graduate program admission. The bottom center portion refers to the constellation of personal communities in which the graduate continues to participate in varying degrees during the course of her/his degree program. Family may include spouses and children as well as other relatives whose expectations and encouragement may support or detract from graduate study. Friends include peers on and off campus. *Employers* refers to job settings that are generally outside the academic program area, though they may include on-campus venues that are not under the control of the academic program area but nonetheless may affect the graduate experience.

The top center portion refers to the professional communities for which the graduate student is preparing. Practitioners serve as role models and participate in the clinical components of graduate degree programs. Professional associations set standards for admission to professional practice and administer examinations for licensing, thereby influencing the nature of academic programs. Finally, the right portion of Figure 4 reflects the primary outcome of the professional socialization process, a novice professional practitioner. It represents the core elements of successful professional socialization, a well developed commitment to and identification with the chosen professional career.

The bottom line in Figure 4 lists the interactive stages of socialization (anticipatory, formal, informal, personal). A linear approach to socialization would associate each stage with a particular component or set of components in Figure 4, for example, anticipatory with prospective students; formal and informal with personal and professional communities, and the university; and personal with novice professional practitioners. We assert, however, that socialization processes characteristic of all four stages may be present at any point in the entire experience of graduate students and novice practitioners. For example, the actions of current students could have an impact on future public policies or on the status of a profession. Professional identity and commitment are not presented in the framework simply as outcomes of a socialization process but are conceived as developing gradually in the individual student, both affecting and being affected by the other components of the framework.

The ellipses in Figure 4 have broken lines to represent the permeable, shifting boundaries among the various conceptual elements. Although the various conceptual elements of socialization have some analytically distinct characteristics, they are not independent but rather dependent upon one another to varying degrees. Consequently, we construe Figure 4 as a dynamic framework that is useful across a variety of academic programs and types of students. Figure 4 thus represents an interactive rather than a solely causal model.

Socialization is dynamic and ongoing, without a definite beginning or end.

Professional identity and commitment are not achieved at some finite level but continue to evolve. Socialization is dynamic and ongoing, without a definite beginning or end. More difficult to illustrate in Figure 4 is the idea that increasing engagement with a set of professional roles (i.e., increasing identification and role commitment) as well as disengagement (i.e., a decision to discontinue graduate preparation) are possible at any point in the socialization process.

The present conceptual framework suggests several aspects of institutional culture that should be addressed in the contemporary context of interactive and reciprocal new and collaborative plans as we strive to enhance the socialization of graduate and professional students. Included among them are supporting student diversity, infusing professional and ethical norms in graduate programs, the challenge of distance education, initiating program modification, and reexamining the faculty role in the socialization process. The next section addresses these aspects of institutional culture and identifies a number of resources available to assist efforts at graduate program reform designed to make professional socialization more interactive and student centered.

Institutional Culture: Recurrent Themes

A DISCUSSION OF THE SOCIALIZATION of graduate and professional students would not be complete without examining recurrent themes and issues that reflect the dynamic nature of the institutional culture underlying graduate education. This section illustrates several of the changing patterns that affect institutional culture and are exerting pressure for reform. It also highlights some of the initiatives under way to improve the experience of graduate and professional students.

Diversity

Historically, women and people of color have either not been represented at all or have been severely underrepresented in the doctoral and professional ranks, either by choice or as a result of the social climate prevailing in those departments and fields. "In some fields—notably psychology, the social sciences, and the life sciences—females are well represented as students but underrepresented in the professoriate and are not always appointed to assistant professor positions at a rate that one would expect on the basis of Ph.D. and postdoctoral student representation. In other fields—such as mathematics, physics, computer science, and engineering—females are underrepresented at all levels. In all fields, the confidence of female students might be low, especially where they are isolated and have few female role models" (Committee on Science, Engineering, and Public Policy, 1997, p. 11).

In 1999, women earned 42.5 percent of all the earned doctorates awarded. The largest proportions of doctorates earned by women were in the fields of education (64 percent) and social sciences (54.3 percent); the smallest were in engineering (14.8 percent), physical sciences (23.3 percent), and business (31 percent). Foreign students were awarded 27.6 percent of all earned doctorates in 1999, with the largest proportions in engineering (48.6 percent) and physical sciences (40.7 percent). Black students received 5.8 percent and Hispanic students 4.2 percent of all earned doctorates in 1999 (Leatherman, 2001).

Since the 1950s, the number of women entering graduate school has steadily increased. Numbers of applicants of color have also increased, but actual percentages compared with majority applications show them to be underrepresented (Turner, Myers, and Creswell, 1999). While minority entrance scores and grade point averages also are on the rise, they are slightly lower than white applicants' scores. Minority attrition has declined only slightly, in part because there are few minorities on the faculty (Johnson, 1983). Historically, the relatively small numbers of women students and faculty members have made support systems nonexistent or tenuous at best (Lopate, 1968). The attrition rate for women has declined in recent years, partly because more women are staying in graduate programs and providing much needed support systems for each other and for newly enrolled women.

One key factor for improving retention of female students is increasing the number of women role models and mentors. Because the socialization of graduate students has been dominated by male faculty members and advisers, more women and advisers of color are needed to facilitate effective socialization for female graduate students (Lopate, 1968). When considering the socialization process faced by women and people of color, one solution would be to bring "the fantasies of gatekeepers and neophytes closer to reality" (Sells, 1975, p. 8).

In the field of law, the proportion of entering female students remained low in the 1960s (3.8 percent in 1963; 6.9 percent in 1969), tripled in the 1970s (9.4 percent in 1970; 31.4 percent in 1979), and continued to grow to 42 percent in 1991–92 (Epstein, 1993, pp. 53, 426). Growth in the proportion of female faculty members has been much slower, with women constituting 24 percent of the full-time faculty in 1990 (Epstein, 1993, p. 434). Over the years, continuous debate has ensued over whether the problem of underrepresentation of women and people of color lies with the graduate education system or centers on individual student preferences (Sells, 1975;

Turner, Myers, and Creswell, 1999). While the qualitative study of sixty-four faculty of color by Turner, Myers, and Creswell (1999) did not focus on the graduate student experience, the institutional climates described by respondents could apply just as well to graduate programs as they did to their subsequent places of academic employment: "A few respondents, 5% of the total, stated that they had not encountered racial and ethnic discrimination as they performed their faculty duties, but most acknowledged continuing racial and ethnic biases in their colleges and universities. Though most faculty, over 95%, said they plan to stay in academe, they repeatedly mentioned the handicaps of isolation, lack of information about tenure and promotion, unsupportive work environments, gender bias, language barriers, lack of mentoring, and lack of support from superiors. They identified racial and ethnic bias as the most troubling challenge they faced in the academic workplace" (p. 41).

While focusing on undergraduate students, Hurtado, Milem, Clayton-Pedersen, and Allen (1999) nonetheless identify several possible effects of the campus climate for diversity that apply equally to graduate students of color: "First, . . . individuals' and particular groups' perceptions of the environment are not inconsequential or intangible, but have tangible and real effects . . . on educational outcomes. Second, many studies indicate the importance of having diverse peers in the learning environment for important outcomes, such as improvements in students' ability to engage in more complex thinking about problems and to consider multiple perspectives. . . . Third, . . . racial conflict can be minimized and learning environments enhanced by diversity" (pp. iv–v).

The ultimate outcomes of socialization vary depending on students' undergraduate and graduate institutions, campus climate, program reputations, and price tag. An academic hierarchy dictates where prospective graduate students can and cannot enter all disciplines and professions (Kerlin, 1995a, 1995b). Some graduate programs serve as filters so that exclusion takes place at every level, causing disproportional distributions among gender and racial groups (Yoder, 1984). If homosocial reproduction is still being practiced (i.e., admitting students who "look like" the faculty), fewer women and minority candidates than men are being accepted, trained, and eventually graduated. Further, the socialization of women and minority graduate students is not likely to resemble that of their male classmates (Turner and Thompson, 1993).

In the field of psychiatry, socialization has historically encompassed the male perspective in doctor-client relationships and overlooked issues that could be affected by a client's race and gender as they relate to illness. Issues related to gender and race pertinent to mental well-being would differ significantly from the socialization of traditional white males that emphasizes how white males relate to female and minority clients (Griffith and Delgado, 1979). Minority candidates in psychiatry also believe they experience a more isolated socialization process than do white residents. The situation may also be hampered by white physicians' reluctance to accept black residents in psychiatry (Griffith and Delgado, 1979).

It is no secret that women and graduate students of color view their experiences differently from their white male counterparts (Ronkowski and Iannaccone, 1989; Turner, Myers, and Creswell, 1999; Willie, Grady, and Hope, 1991; Blackwell, 1987). A longitudinal study of all students entering the three medical schools in North Carolina in 1975 who were followed up in 1978–79 identified the following patterns of gender differences in socialization:

> *When compared with males, females started medical school somewhat more oriented to humanitarian patient-care values, political and economic change in medicine, the problems facing women physicians and patients, and inner-city ghetto practice. These differences initially were due partially to women's greater nurturance, lower interest in money, and greater liberalism. The sex difference on liberalism was by far the best explanation for the initial sex variations in professional orientations. . . . Blacks, another minority in medicine, are also more liberal on a variety of issues.*
>
> *Despite the increased conservatism of all students over time, most initial orientation differences between the sexes persisted and a few new ones emerged . . . [with] women leaving school more oriented to equalizing doctor/patient interactions and men more interested in volunteer work and rural practice. The sexes also appeared to slightly polarize on some questions of sex discrimination, so that the initial sex differences widened on these issues. [Leserman, 1981, p. 95]*

Because socialization and training norms revolve around a white male standard, out-group members (in this case, women and minorities) may well regard their instruction and expectations as unrealistic by comparison (Griffith and Delgado, 1979). For instance, female students experience limited attention to their needs, possible sexual harassment, and fewer opportunities than those taken for granted by male classmates (Kerlin, 1995a). Women reported having to try harder than their male counterparts, having their work overlooked and not taken seriously, and having faculty presume their work will be of lesser quality than men's (Lopate, 1968). Women also found less support for their interests and ideas than did the men. Women and minorities often miss being escorted to the gate by well connected white, male faculty (Yoder, 1984; Valverde and Brown, 1988). In short, what has been asserted for women in education administration is applicable to women and minorities in many other professional fields: "different organizational incentives . . . make for different patterns of socialization, both in process and results" (Ortiz and Marshall, 1998, p. 131).

One midwestern study compared the experiences of white and nonwhite women graduate students (Turner and Thompson, 1993). White women tended to describe their graduate environments as cooperative, collaborative, and collegial; nonwhite women used words such as competitive, uncollegial, and isolated to describe their perceptions. Majority women were more likely to have mentors than minority women. The researchers found gender disparities to be magnified by racial discrimination. Consequently, white women were more skilled at participating in professional activities that socialized them for networking, presenting scholarly work, and coauthoring manuscripts than were their nonwhite female classmates (Turner and Thompson, 1993).

In school administration programs, women often believe they may not be receiving the same encouragement as men to pursue graduate work. Men, by contrast, are encouraged more, obtain more counseling, choose effective role models in the field, choose to be administrators earlier in their career, and thus enroll in graduate programs sooner than women and minority candidates (Oller, 1979; Ortiz and Marshall, 1988). Even when they get to graduate school, women often feel disadvantaged in comparison to their male counterparts: "A predominantly male faculty results in a lack of role models for women students, thus depriving them of the inspiration to advance and the assurance that they can succeed. The 'male locker-room network,' from which women students are excluded, still exists. Women miss out on the informal mentoring inherent in this system and have weaker advancement and career opportunities because this internal communication channel provides many relevant pieces of career advice to male students" (Nerad and Cerny, 1999, p. 4).

Biracial and multiracial groups of students are also searching for their own identities and voices on campus. These students challenge patterns of socialization in graduate academic programs as they develop personal identities while simultaneously "promoting cross-racial dialogue" to reduce racial hostility on campus (Renn, 2000, p. 416). Biracial and multiracial graduate students struggle to find faculty role models and mentors who share their heritage.

As another example, early in psychology graduate programs, men and women are deemed equal players in the degree pursuit. Both groups are "passively deferential and externally evaluated" (Sells, 1975, p. 10). The movement to ABD status forces students to assume a new identity where "publishing, networking, and presenting . . . [take] confidence, assertiveness, and the support of mentors" (p. 10). A woman tends to experience greater concern in this role as it challenges her confidence level and deepens her need for female role models and mentors, of which there have been few.

International Graduate Students

International student populations, especially in the natural science fields, have risen dramatically over the past four decades. Between 1958 and 1988, the number of non-U.S. residents receiving Ph.D.s from American universities increased from 772 to 8,589 (Bowen and Rudenstine, 1992, p. 28). In some major research institutions, more than half the graduate assistants are not from the United States (Kulik, 1985). While faculty may have time to devote to honing the research skills of international graduate students, faculty are less likely to spend time working on the teaching skills of those international students who are teaching assistants. The international students who find themselves in teaching roles may not be as well prepared for the academic profession in terms of language, culture, or pedagogical training to succeed in the classroom as are their research assistant peers who are prepared for research in the lab (Smith, 1993). Many faculty members find it difficult to deal with cultural differences in interaction patterns and hence concentrate on academic matters rather than on other aspects of professional socialization. As a result, international students are often forced to turn to peers for support and encouragement as well as for assistance with problems of adapting to American life and culture. Faculty may assume that some students will enter research positions for which they will be prepared or that many will return to their native country where norms and expectations will vary considerably from those in the United States (Smith, 1993).

Professionalism

A culminating outcome of the graduate and professional socialization process is an orientation toward professionalism that elevates the holder of a specialized body of knowledge to a position that characteristically receives certain esteem, benefits, and privileges (Bledstein, 1976). Socialization to professionalism "requires changes in students' self-images, attitudes, and thinking processes" (Egan, 1989, p. 201). Faculty-student roles and interactions are transformed (Egan, 1989). The pinnacle to which students aspired is often described as "the sphere of the sacred and the charismatic" (Bledstein, 1976, p. 90), a very mystical world with a language and value system all its own that must become real, penetrable, and achievable to the graduate student. The gatekeepers "controlled the magic circle of scientific knowledge [that] only the few, specialized by training and indoctrination, were privileged to enter" but whom all others were "obligated to appreciate" (p. 90).

Professionals also control the flow of information and the direction of research in their specialized body of knowledge. By setting admission practices, retention of students, mentoring, and sponsorship for employment, established professionals regulate which (and how many) new professionals will be brought into the field (Ohmann, 1990). In the case of medicine and education, state government controls certification and licensure; in other cases, professional boards sanction practice. For the arts and sciences, the dissertation defense and job placement mark the passage to acceptance by academe.

For certain professional programs such as medicine, social work, and educational administration, socialization begins in the classroom but ends in the hospital, clinical setting, or school building. Perhaps one concern is that the socialization process prepares students to be successful in the student role played out in the university department but does not adequately prepare incumbents to be professional practitioners, although professional socialization is often unrealistically described and promised in the mission statements of graduate programs (Quarantelli, Helfrich, and Yutsy, 1964). As a result, socialization is segmented and compartmentalized. Students must eventually shed the low autonomy they once had in the classroom for the higher autonomy that prevails in the applied setting. Clearly, professionalism begins at different points for each profession.

In the medical setting, the socialization of medical students is affected more by interaction with patients, personal revelation, and daily presence in the hospital than by faculty mentoring (Hafferty and Franks, 1994; Olmstead and Paget, 1969). As students experience the practice of medicine in hospitals and are socialized into its cognitive and affective dimensions, they gain self-confidence and maturity, becoming more serious minded, self-directed, responsible, and realistic (Coombs, 1978).

Professional identity also comes from successfully negotiating the key rites of passage and securing recognizable status symbols. For medical students, it includes responsibility for hospital patients. In turn, the role of physician becomes further internalized when recognition of one's new position comes from other hospital personnel (Coombs, 1978). For the doctoral student, identity can be derived from admission to candidacy, successful defense of the dissertation, and publication of research.

Previous experience and critical incidents during socialization affect professionalism. Prior exposure to a field enhances self-concept as students have an opportunity to shadow and work with professionals in a professional setting. For example, those entering the clergy usually have prior exposure to the established church; likewise, educational administrators begin their careers as teachers. In contrast to graduate students' pursuing degrees in educational administration or the arts and sciences, prospective physicians and lawyers (especially) do not have the same opportunity for early exposure to the professional realm (Pavalko and Holley, 1974). The culture of professionalism forms from a combination of "internships, professional oaths, ordination, association meetings, scholarly papers, awards and prizes, [and] recognition . . . of elders" (Bledstein, 1976, p. 94).

Each ritual or ceremony not only signifies to the student a transformation and acceptance into the hallowed body of scholars but also signifies to the general public that the graduate has earned the rights and privileges associated with professional practice and should thus be accorded a full and practicing membership in the profession (Bledstein, 1976). Unfortunately, the status of all professions is not equal. Those professions occupying the top of the hierarchy typically have elaborate rituals, transmit an esoteric body of knowledge, hold authority over other fields, command great respect in service to clients, and tend to be accorded greater status from society (Bledstein, 1976).

For instance, for academic graduates in the arts and sciences, the conferring university, thickness of one's portfolio, quality of the assistantship, length of the resume, number of presentations, number and locations of published articles in respected, refereed journals, and reputation of the chair of one's dissertation committee all speak to one's professional status (Bledstein, 1976). Similarly, board certification, passage of the bar exam, and state licensure elevate the medical, law, and educational administration professional to practicing status (Bledstein, 1976).

Professionalism, however, is not merely a matter of externally recognized accomplishment but also involves the internal acceptance of a value system indicative of the newly accepted role. Socialization toward professionalism becomes a synthesis of knowledge about facts and about behavioral expectations of the role "into a coherent and consistent behavioral pattern" commonly associated with members of that field or profession (Knight, 1973, p. 4).

> **Professionalism . . . is not merely a matter of externally recognized accomplishment but also involves the internal acceptance of a value system indicative of the newly accepted role.**

Professionalization

Professionalism is accomplished through a carefully structured professionalization process that revolves around students' immersion into an environment that exacts or is prototypical of the one to which the student aspires (Mann, 1994). Professionalization rarely occurs in the classroom but is more likely to evolve from on-the-job training and experiences (Blackburn and Fox, 1976). The goal is not necessarily knowledge acquisition alone but the normative control of members. It is also "the inculcation of a professional ethic to safeguard the members from inevitable mistakes that will someday be made on the job" (p. 809). As a result, the major testing of on-the-job endurance for doctors and lawyers comes after graduation from professional school rather than before. Professional status has already been bestowed without more consistent reality checkpoints. In the arts and sciences, by contrast, status is awarded after satisfactory demonstration and evaluation of salient knowledge of subject matter and skill in research and to a lesser extent, teaching (Olmstead and Paget, 1969). In the arts and sciences, however, the degree of expectation is not standardized and thus varies from discipline to discipline and by dissertation committee.

The milieu from which the degree is awarded (university, department and faculty reputation, quality of the dissertation committee) affects the professionalization process such that some graduates will be better prepared for their profession than others (Mann, 1994). Degrees from top-rated institutions and internships from prestigious locations will also influence the professionalization process.

Faculty are instrumental in helping to prepare advisees for professional roles (Hockin, 1981) as reflected in what emphasis they place on the adviser as role model and mentor to students (Mann, 1994), how well they help students fulfill occupational roles (McFarland and Caplow, 1995; Ronkowski and Iannaccone, 1989), how well they synthesize the graduate and professional degree program experience (Hockin, 1981), and how clearly they transmit professional values (Hockin, 1981). Graduate students themselves are expected by faculty and nonacademic professional practitioners to actively pursue knowledge, reflect the acceptable and prevailing value system, work well with faculty, and develop critical thinking ability to be accorded professional status (Mann, 1994).

Ethics

Acceptance of a professional identity implies acceptance of the ethical principles associated with professional practice. The skills and knowledge acquired by new professionals are augmented by the standards and acceptable values and behaviors that "act as moral constraints upon their behavior in the absence of external controls" (Caplovitz, 1980, p. 3). Under careful faculty tutelage, doctoral students use proper research techniques. Under the watchful eye of the practicing physician, medical interns learn proper surgical technique. Although ethics may be relegated to the hidden curriculum in graduate school, students learn to follow sound ethical judgment in research, teaching, and clinical practice by observing role models and mentors (Folse, 1991). Largely, however, ethical principles form in some measure during one's lifelong socialization process and are strengthened or become more focused only during graduate training (Becker, Geer, Hughes, and Strauss, 1961). For the most part, past ethical training is not always formalized in the curriculum (Killingsworth and Twale, 1993; Stover, 1989), addressed to the extent needed to effect public trust (Forsyth and Danisiewicz, 1985), or prominent enough to alter significantly students' views, especially in the medical and legal professions (Keenan, Brown, Pontell, and Geis, 1985).

Technology and Distance Learning

With changing student demographic patterns among undergraduates, tighter budgets, and smaller faculties, graduate and professional programs are experimenting with various technologies and distance learning formats. Changes in students' ages, gender ratios, ethnic backgrounds, single and multiple disabilities, learning styles, proximity to campus programs, and personal and work commitments and circumstances have necessitated concomitant accommodations in program and instructional delivery with the proviso that a program's viability and integrity be maintained (Thompson, 1998). Porter (1997) indicated that distance learning, while not a panacea for everyone or all educational programs, is a critical link in the education of students with special needs and circumstances.

Audio, video, compact disk, and other computer technologies integrated into formal classroom settings have been transformed or evolved into wired campuses, distance learning formats, and virtual universities. Technology, whether in the classroom or from the virtual campus, offers new teaching tools such as computer simulations and CD-ROM applications that enhance and often revolutionize courses, especially those in the sciences and medicine. Access to on-line knowledge databases augments and expedites the physical holdings of the campus library for uses in research and publication. With increased student diversity, the tools available and the possibilities for instructional delivery continue to expand (Anderson and Garrison, 1998). While these new pedagogical approaches and resources fulfill students' desires for low cost, practicality, proximity, and convenience, however, most of these innovations fail to address the face-to-face faculty/student and student/peer social exchanges common to the formal classroom and integral to professional socialization.

While technological advances have permeated classrooms and affected the production and dissemination of knowledge, technology has not as yet revolutionized basic educational contexts or replaced books, professors, chalk, and erasers (Gumport and Chun, 1999). The impact of technology on delivery of educational content has necessitated a reexamination of faculty and student roles as they relate to learning. Because technology can overcome geographic and temporal limitations on students' participation in courses, graduate students in distance education programs may not be experiencing the same elements as their counterparts in traditional, on-campus programs. This situation affects how graduate teaching assistants are prepared for the virtual classroom of tomorrow and for the possibilities that technology may spawn.

Of even greater import is the need for students to become socialized into their profession and prepare for the professional role. For instance, much of the traditional face-to-face interaction between on-campus students and faculty provides a mechanism by which faculty assess students' ability, capability, and ultimate fitness for the profession. Fulfilling the gatekeeping function, normal mentoring duties, and direct supervision of research would be more difficult for faculty using distance education. These functions are not totally impossible in distance education, but the distance modality does tend to bypass the richness normally found in these common interpersonal academic relationships. While distance education may satisfy the teaching function reasonably well, its ability to develop and hone research, professional practice, application skills, and professionalism remains unconvincing. Zeller (1995) identified four models of distance education (laissez-faire, consortium, coordinating board, and comprehensive) in an effort to categorize distinct formats of delivery that ensure nonduplicated, time-saving, cost-effective, accessible education to students. While this study addressed certain policy implications, it lacked a discussion of distance education's impact on professional socialization. Virtual education presents challenges that include addressing and reconstructing two-way classroom interaction, capturing meaningful classroom dialogue, and encouraging important aspects of professional development such as mentoring, research, presenting, and networking (Anderson and Garrison, 1998; Gatz and Hirt, 2000).

Reticence and lack of support can further stifle technology-based programs. Learning new roles for faculty and graduate students, in addition to keeping pace with technology while not appearing faddish, poses additional challenges (Anderson and Garrison, 1998). Faculty cyber-competence and cyber-receptivity have often failed to keep pace with technological expansions, thus relegating technological adaptation and distance learning to a few academic areas. In terms of graduate and professional education, a balance would need to be reached to ensure the most effective means of transmitting electronic knowledge while guaranteeing that professional competence derived from the graduate student socialization process is not compromised or diminished (Porter, 1997). The next section addresses similarities and differences in socialization across graduate degree fields.

Institutional Culture and Socialization: Differences Among Academic Programs

CHARACTERISTICS OF INDIVIDUAL GRADUATE and professional programs have as many similarities as differences across the core elements of socialization shown in Table 1 (knowledge acquisition, investment, and involvement) and the stages of socialization (anticipatory, formal, informal, and personal). Disciplines and professional fields also vary according to the structural engagement of graduate students and the resulting development of identity with and commitment to corresponding professional roles. Variations appear in such areas as organizational structures, program processes, professional standards, admission standards, examinations and other rites of passage, curricula, faculty role and supervision, and student peer culture. Using the basic dimensions shown in Table 1 and reflected in Figure 4, this section provides examples to highlight similarities and differences in graduate preparation and practice for medicine, dentistry, law, and theology; master's and doctoral level professional programs in educational administration, public administration, social work, business, architecture, library science, and engineering; and doctoral programs in arts and sciences disciplines.

Knowledge Acquisition

Knowledge acquisition encompasses the student's ability to understand and acclimate to the academic culture, to meet faculty standards, and to perform role expectations after being provided with both basic and advanced information. This information can be obtained through formal and informal means from a variety of sources, primarily academic structures and standards, faculty role and supervision, and the student peer culture. Knowledge acquisition comes mainly from organizational structures (with faculty serving as primary socializing agents) and student peer culture.

Organizational Structures

Aspects of the campus organizational structure (particularly the mission, faculty credentials, academic requirements, departmental characteristics, and reputation) influence students' socialization (Stark, Lowther, Hagerty, and Orczyk, 1986). The esprit or ethos of individual academic and professional departments serves as a frame of reference for newly entering graduate students and lays a foundation for socialization into the field represented. In addition to meeting with faculty and current students, graduate students can also use catalog and Web resources to access information about the program and its normative context. Students may observe internal politics of the graduate program, what is valued within the department, and key interaction patterns, thereby building their knowledge of faculty and their future profession from these images.

The structure of each discipline or field encourages various student responses based on normative expectations and valued outcomes. For instance, in the classroom, arts and sciences disciplines follow models of acceptance and respect for the professoriat, while the assertive model is encouraged in law school classrooms (Wolensky, 1976). Humanities fields often prepare graduate students in teaching rather than research, placing some graduates at a disadvantage if they secure employment at a research university (Cahn, 1986). Sociology graduate students are asked to learn an ever expanding body of knowledge yet are forced to bring closure through a synthesis achieved in the dissertation phase of their program (Wolensky, 1976).

Graduate students also become aware of intellectual ethnocentrism, that is, learning where their discipline fits in with others across campus, where their program stands nationally, and who among faculty in the program are respected and esteemed in the department and in the field. The choice of a particular graduate program is important, because its rank strongly influences the future of the graduate. Lower-ranked departments rarely see their graduates enter positions in higher-ranked research institutions or departments

(Breneman, 1975), despite the fact that "professional education programs are relatively homogeneous and single-goal oriented" (Bragg, 1976, p. 32). Faculty reputation, as reflected in national reports (Goldberger, Maher, and Flattau, 1995) and influential periodicals (for example, *U.S. News & World Report*) permits prospective and current graduate students to select whom to admire and whose values to emulate (Caplovitz, 1980). On the negative side, graduate students may not recognize that they are taking on and perpetuating faculty perspectives that are rigid and passé (Thompson, 1978).

Socialization is also affected by the pecking order among and within disciplines. Breneman (1975) conducted site visits to fourteen research universities over a six-year period, gathering statistical documents from numerous government and campus sources, enrollment trends, and job placement data for arts and sciences and engineering graduates. He found that research assistantships and fellowships tend to be more prestigious for students than teaching assistantships (in large part because of the greater probability of having published something before entering a faculty role), thus creating differences in student socialization processes within disciplines as well as among them. The availability of such experiences is in turn related to departmental quality. Consequently, it is not surprising that graduates of more highly regarded departments are often sought to raise the standing of lower-ranked departments (Breneman, 1975).

> **Socialization is also affected by the pecking order among and within disciplines.**

Program Structures

The structure of various graduate and professional programs differs by profession. Graduate students study under faculty supervision and learn the role of professor early in their socialization. In a landmark study of medical school classes, Becker, Geer, Hughes, and Strauss (1961) used participant observation and conducted formal and informal interviews of faculty and fifteen students from each of the four classes to characterize the medical school culture and students' perspectives of that culture. They found medical school students to lack career role models until they progress toward the clinical stages of their schooling.

Blackburn and Fox (1976) concluded, in their study of 350 medical school faculty, that those with the Ph.D. were more easily socialized into academe and the faculty role than medical school faculty who held only the M.D. While the Ph.D. graduate tends to move from one academic environment into another, M.D. graduates move into hospitals and medical practice centers for further training as interns and residents.

Programs differ in terms of whether they provide clear structure or vague approximations to their students, socialize them in cohort groupings or as individuals, or practice passive versus active, visible socialization. Pease's quantitative study of doctoral students (1967) emphasized professional interaction and the importance of faculty encouragement on students' professionalization into the field. While academic socialization in the arts and sciences tends to begin with cohort socialization and conclude with the one-on-one, faculty-to-student format, the medical profession socializes incumbents using more collective techniques in class and through clinical and residency experiences.

While the differences in curricular content across fields are obvious, the instructional delivery of that curriculum most assuredly sets the tone for how students are socialized into that profession. For instance, from an extensive, landmark study of Columbia Law School surveying 926 students and employing participant observation of one class from matriculation through graduation, Thielens (1980) concluded that competitiveness rather than cooperation was encouraged. In another longitudinal study, Kay (1978) questioned law students about the impact of values on role behavior and the degree of heterogeneity of value formation among the lawyers as a group. She determined that legal education focuses on case analysis and precedent, not the formation of accepted professional values and beliefs (see also Epstein, 1993, and Stover, 1989). Because faculty are consumed with a need to transmit knowledge and evaluate the acquisition of skills, the essential values, ethics, attitudes, and beliefs of the profession are often relegated to a minimally essential status in the university law curriculum (Olmsted and Paget, 1969).

Faculty Role and Supervision

Because faculty are expected to select and assess the performance of graduate students as part of their gatekeeping function, paternalism is sometimes evident. Faculty as gatekeepers hold the ascribed duty of regulating who will and who will not be granted entry into a graduate program. They determine who shall be privy to the closely guarded body of knowledge they possess as well as which graduate students shall be anointed and certified as qualified to engage in professional practice. In the arts and sciences especially, faculty members tend to remain in sole control of the student's fate. Through interviews with forty-eight students over two years, Bucher and Stellings (1977) examined how the graduate academic program molds trainees into professionals. They suggested that the linear structure of a doctoral program, by forcing faculty-student pairings, gives students little opportunity to explore alternatives or to take personal destiny into their own hands.

Further, if the student's philosophical perspective is not congruent with the faculty's normative images of the field or discipline, the student is likely to leave the program (Wright, 1967). Wright observed that joining a professional association was a positive step toward solidifying professional engagement. Committed students were those whose prior image of the discipline was more congruent with the professional model, in the case of sociology, adapted by the department. The willingness of incongruent graduate students to change their perspective and fulfill faculty expectations, while probable, is not always wholehearted.

Faculty advisers may explain norms of organizational expectations quite clearly to their advisees, but not necessarily all of their peers may get similar information, a situation that can create dissonance for the student. Some students are able to adapt to organizational norms more easily than others, perhaps because of personality characteristics or more accurate anticipatory socialization (Gallagher, Hossler, Catania, and Kolman, 1986). Those who do not adapt usually exit the program voluntarily or by faculty and administrative request.

For science fields such as biochemistry, the rigorous standards of coursework serve as a sorting mechanism. In addition, students are encouraged to write and deliver research papers and perform undergraduate teaching to be accorded the role of biochemist. Their socialization conveys a series of messages that not only foretell their future in the profession but also strongly encourage them to embrace the concomitant values and beliefs associated with the field that are modeled by the faculty (Bucher and Stellings, 1977).

In an eight-week pilot project and follow-up questionnaire of twenty-four women in arts, sciences, education, and nursing, Sells (1975) studied problems women face in graduate school. Her respondents indicated that sorting and selecting procedures flourish through poor faculty advising and indifference to students (for example, excluding some students, or showing favoritism based on gender, race, or some other factor). She suggested that faculty often exercise gatekeeping functions by withholding informal guidelines to students that govern certain aspects of protocol in the program. Her respondents felt that faculty perpetuate paternalism toward students. Many lack coherent and consistent expectations of their students. As a result, faculty may foster a culture of alienation, playing up the obvious powerlessness of students (Sells, 1975).

Students learn to conform to their professors' beliefs and the normative expectations of their program and, at the very least, passively accept faculty ideology and world views. Weinholtz (1991) explored teamwork patterns among sixty-two medical students on rounds using observation, participant observation, and interviews. Results indicated that the norm is to accept the existing paradigm, not change it; upsetting the status quo is neither valued nor rewarded (see also Thompson, 1978). While faculty may pay lip service to training creative, independent thinkers, the socializing pattern indicates that they tend to graduate those students who reflect their own scholarly work and professional ideology (Thompson, 1978). For instance, incumbents often spend time decoding professional and faculty expectations rather than focusing on the lessons learned from viewing their program, discipline, and professional expectations in a more holistic fashion (Rosen and Bates, 1967).

Faculty should supply the neophyte with a consistent and clear process that facilitates socialization. Although some information is communicated formally, explicitly, and periodically, less formal knowledge is not always transmitted with much precision (Rosen and Bates, 1967). For example, in their interviews of forty senior arts and sciences faculty, McFarland and Caplow (1995) identified three types of investments faculty make while supervising doctoral students—interpersonal, social psychological, and occupational. Much ambiguity emerges, in large part because of how faculty sustain the culture or environment.

Essentially, what students receive depends on "the rules the faculty make, the way the faculty [organize] and [define] the situation in which students must perform, and the way faculty [interpret] and [apply] their rules and definitions" (Becker, Geer, Hughes, and Strauss, 1961, p. 48). Whether faculty develop a culture of contradiction and defeat depends on the extent to which they favor autonomy over paternalism and encourage students' initiative (Becker, Geer, Hughes, and Strauss, 1961; Caplovitz, 1980; McFarland and Caplow, 1995). In the case of medical students, they are closely supervised and accorded only very limited autonomy (Becker, Geer, Hughes, and Strauss, 1961).

Medical education is notorious for inundating students with massive amounts of information, far too much for any student to master completely. Consequently, medical students struggle collectively to discover how much of what types of knowledge must be learned to get by (Becker, Geer, Hughes, and Strauss, 1961). A more recent ethnographic study of the McMaster University Medical School in Canada (Haas and Shaffir, 1987) suggests that little has changed in this area and several others (for example, students' anxiety about future responsibilities, uncertainty with respect to diagnosis and rapidly changing treatment approaches, faculty-centered instruction) over the years since the groundbreaking study by Becker, Geer, Hughes, and Strauss (1961). Even changes in student composition and curricular innovation (for example, introduction of problem-based approaches) have failed to alleviate the intense pressure on students: "Medical students in both traditional programs and the innovative program we observed are uncertain about the relevance of their curricula to the demands they will face as professionals. Both groups are also dubious about the effectiveness of their respective evaluation processes. In this context of ambiguity, students in both settings accommodate themselves, individually and collectively, to convincing others of their developing competence by selective learning and by striving to control the impressions others receive of them" (Haas and Shaffir, 1987, p. 52).

In contrast, graduate teaching assistants have varying degrees of freedom and autonomy, depending on the discipline and department. In a study of 364 teaching assistants at a major research institution, Pavalko and

Holley (1974) explored the notion of professional self-concept and role enactment in terms of students' degree of freedom and autonomy. They found that the complexity of graduate teaching assistants' work and how closely it related to what faculty actually do increased their professional self-concepts. Perceived success in the teaching assistant role also increased autonomy and promoted professional self-concept.

Student Peer Culture

As neophytes prepare to be members of a professional community, they assimilate into the informal student peer culture (Rosen and Bates, 1967). Entering graduate or professional school with a group of other students affects the socialization process differently from entering individually. The cohort influences the learning process, opens support mechanisms, and enriches the experience socially and emotionally. Through observation, scales, psychological tests, and interviews of 229 medical students over four years, Coombs (1978) determined that when students are admitted because they share similarities, the bond is likely to be stronger than when their characteristics are diverse. Group homogeneity eases students into the new culture, increases peer solidarity, and initially decreases identification with faculty (Caplovitz, 1980).

Peer solidarity also dispels the "culture of silence," the anxiety manifest in preparing to assume uncharted career direction (Slevin, 1992) and a peer affirmation that students had chosen the "right field." Students also need to feel a part of the social fabric of a department through organized activities as well as common academic interests. Interviewing twenty-nine teaching assistants in arts and sciences, business, and engineering, Kirk and Todd-Mancillas (1991) reported findings similar to McFarland and Caplow (1995), describing three professional teaching assistant identities: intellectual, socioemotional, and occupational. In addition, they found teaching assistants desire and need to see faculty model professionalism.

While university departments can supply students with formal information, classmates fill in the remainder (Staton and Darling, 1989). Student culture also affords members opportunities to view the informal aspects of their chosen profession. As they enter and progress through their program, students use several strategies to gather information: passive observation, passive listening or eavesdropping, active listening, interactive sharing of perceptions, and testing interpretations of perceptions. Perhaps the most common need for information is about faculty behavior, because students are reluctant to consult faculty directly and thus limit interaction to benign topics, such as plans of study and assignment clarification (Staton and Darling, 1989). Early in the program, graduate students wrestle with departmental and university policy and procedures. Rather than ask faculty, student peers ask each other their interpretations and what concomitant behavior should then follow (Staton and Darling, 1989). Even though in certain facets of program expectations faculty advisers are the likely source of information, often a peer who has just hurdled a significant obstacle in the program is a more likely source of encouragement and support than a faculty member (Staton and Darling, 1989).

In conjunction with peer appraisals, student self-assessment varies across disciplines as well. In the course of a graduate program, students receive direct and indirect cues from administrators, faculty, peers, supervisors, and clinicians as to their class standing or professional status. While the arts, humanities, sciences, law, and some of the other master's level professions rely on high grades on examinations and term papers as positive feedback, medical students often regard the absence of negative feedback as a sign they are performing adequately. These medical school self-assessments are critical means by which students gauge their progress. Some medical students, however, disregard negative cues or rationalize them away; other students consider the source and dismiss the criticism (Bucher and Stellings, 1977).

Investment

The degree of time and energy that graduate students put forth in meeting program requirements most closely approximates the extent of investment. As students progress beyond matriculation, enroll in courses, interact with faculty and peers, learn the ropes, and proceed through each semester, their investment deepens. Eventually, there is no turning back, and progression to the ultimate goal appears cemented. Investment increases largely as a result of faculty and student interaction as the student reaches to meet faculty standards and expectations.

Each student passing through a master's or doctoral program may experience the journey differently from other classmates, however, despite the fact that they may have the same schedule. For instance, in some of the master's level professions, students may have work experience and thus may have greater insight into prospective professional roles than young novices entering programs directly after college graduation. For professions such as social work, theology, educational administration, and public administration, students enter at all ages and various stages in their career and personal development. As a result of their varying stages of adult development, students have dissimilar needs and expectations and make different contributions to their programs (Erikson, 1968; Arnett, 2000).

Changing a career or wishing to be promoted in a current one may aid the nontraditionally aged student to move toward more mature professional closure than would be the case for students in their early 20s. Although seasoned nontraditional students possess similar anxieties at admission to those of younger novices, their maturity level supports a socialization process that is distinctly different from what is experienced by their much younger counterparts. More important, the mature group often comes with "baggage" and experiences that add color and interest to the classroom, something that may be absent from a more age homogeneous entering class of recent traditionally aged undergraduates (Levinson, 1978).

Organizational Structures

Departments "differ considerably on the nature and stringency of the demands" placed on new students (Rosen and Bates, 1967, p. 79). Some departments lockstep students through a graduate program (law, medicine, or dentistry, for example), while other academic programs permit a student to postpone key rites of passage, take a semester off to reflect on his or her progress, or continue to prolong his or her tenure by using the individual to cover undergraduate classes or gather data for faculty research projects. This laissez-faire attitude proves more detrimental than beneficial to the student, as he/she prolongs the ordeal of studenthood and postpones the often intimidating role of professional (Rosen and Bates, 1967).

Stark, Lowther, Hagerty, and Orczyk (1986) surveyed 2,217 faculty in 732 professional programs at 346 colleges covering law, medicine, architecture, engineering, library science, business, and liberal arts. They determined that internal influences in professional programs include program and curricular design and content; teaching strategies; and faculty composition, interests, and research emphasis. These internal influences affect the socialization of the graduate student and the quality and marketability of the graduate in terms of such outcomes as technical competence and skills, conceptual or theoretical competence, integrative competence or professional judgment, competence in understanding the various contexts in which the profession exists, competence in adjusting to a changing profession over time, and interpersonal communication (Stark, Lowther, Hagerty, and Orczyk, 1986).

Professional Standards

Entry into a professional area is an experience shared by a select few. While the largest part of selection rests with the novice's choice among alternatives, the keys to the gate are delicately guarded by academics and practicing professionals. The professions of law and medicine, often shrouded in mystery, are more difficult to penetrate than some of the other professions. Nevertheless, each discipline and profession practices one or more sorting and selecting functions (or rituals), from admission through professional practice.

A characteristic that separates some professions from others is the entrance examination. Such an exam attempts to predict future successes while assessing innate ability. The exam, along with previous undergraduate schooling, constitutes a sorting and selecting mechanism that renders an incoming class more homogeneous in expectation than composition. Previous schooling can aid the socialization process, especially if it is in the same field as the graduate program. In professional fields where graduate students come from a variety of undergraduate majors, however, socialization can be much more diffuse.

Daresh and Playko (1995) conducted an extensive review of the literature and the research in educational administration to determine whether career development in this area could borrow from the professional social patterns of lawyers, physicians, or clergy. They found that one professional program, theology, unlike the Ph.D., medical, or law fields, acknowledged a heterogeneous grouping of incumbents, who tended to come from varied undergraduate schools, disciplines, and socioeconomic levels. In addition, specialized entrance examinations do not exist specifically for entrance to theological seminaries as they do for law, medical, and business schools (Daresh and Playko, 1995).

In law school, grades serve as a gatekeeping function, allowing students entry into more prestigious arenas that can serve to enhance their socialization. Higher grades translate to greater occupational development, possibly enabling the student to serve on the university's law review, clerk in a law office for remuneration, or secure a permanent position in a prestigious law firm. Lower grades and placement in a law class mean socialization would be limited to the law classroom (Stover, 1989; Thielens, 1980). Other than grades in law school, students often receive little feedback and thus closely monitor their behavior and class standing in comparison with their peers (Stover, 1989).

As mentioned, professional preparation fields such as law, medicine, and dentistry are likely to have a prescribed, sequential curricular content that limits certain courses to lower- versus upper-level students and solidifies the sequential nature of socialization. Students must often also take specific courses to pass licensure examinations. Doctoral students in the arts and sciences, and to a lesser extent in the professions of business and social work, are freer to chose a plan of study slightly or vastly different from a classmate. Content of and procedures for oral and written examinations may also vary by student, depending on the area of concentration and the composition of the examining committee.

Faculty Role and Expectations

Faculty play a primary role in the socialization of graduate and professional students. They have a major responsibility for shaping a professional self-image that is presumably congruent with a student's total self (Ohmann, 1990). The faculty adviser may also serve as a social control, a gatekeeper who sanctions students' entry into the professional realm. Many advising relationships maintain an almost sacred quality that will rarely be challenged by others.

Most faculty advise as they were advised during their own graduate student career. Consequently, socialization differs, depending on the individual styles of faculty members. General patterns exhibited by advisers can include autocratic and exploitative, autonomous and superficial guidance, benevolent and active in the student's career development, or formal and contractual with their advisee (Hockin, 1981). Ultimately the faculty-student advising relationship is "the social process that transforms the judgmental relationship into a partnership" forming a covenant or collaborative bond signaling faculty recognition of the student's intellectual and research competency (Hockin, 1981, p. 128).

Because there is no one best way of advising graduate students and the process is largely unsupervised, experiences differ by adviser and student. This variability may also be attributed to the extensiveness of faculty advising loads, range of faculty advising experience, or individual advising styles that cover a range from rigid and unapproachable to flexibile, collegial, and collaborative (Hockin, 1981). Socialization of the more academically adept students, whose ideas and interests more closely match those of their advisers, tends to be categorically different from that experienced by the marginal graduate student whose interests do not coincide with her/his adviser's. As a result, time spent together, devotion to program completion, and mutual respect and praise tend ultimately to benefit the academically adept graduate student. For marginal graduate students, interaction with the adviser is likely to be severely limited and not particularly helpful for either professional or personal development (Brown and Krager, 1985).

While students must be conversant with the scope of material covered in the course phase of a graduate program, the road to the doctoral dissertation requires thorough knowledge of a specialized topic, independent thought, and close supervision by the faculty dissertation chair (Cahn, 1986). For many doctoral students, especially those who are not working as research assistants on faculty or departmental projects, formulating a dissertation topic is the most difficult part of their degree program, in large part because it marks the first time in which faculty have not established the types of specific requirements or time lines commonly provided for completing courses.

In most academic disciplines, students are required to perform some independent scholarly research before embarking on a dissertation, and, in the process, they realize the importance of being able to work closely with one or more professors or mentors on their research (Duster, 1987). Within each discipline, alignment with the right faculty member can ensure systematic progress toward the goal of graduation and successful job placement afterward. Not having this sort of alignment can lead to considerable difficulty for the graduate student in ever completing the dissertation, let alone movement into a successful professional career (Borawski, 1987; Ryan, 1987). In many professional fields, doctoral students have more haphazard preparation for the independent research required in a dissertation and, hence, have a greater struggle in formulating a topic.

To use biochemistry as an example of what happens in many other academic disciplines, the choice or assignment of a faculty adviser can be critical to the socialization process and a student's success. The selection of an adviser is often based on common research interests and, perhaps, compatible personality between faculty member and student. Assignment of an adviser, however, tends to be controlled by faculty members who choose their advisees during the admission phase based on reviews of application materials that provide information for assessing the applicant's capacity to contribute to ongoing funded research projects that will be the source of financial support for the student's graduate degree program. In most instances, the decision is not subject to change because financial support depends on the adviser's projects. In addition, to dissolve a student-faculty relationship causes great emotional upheaval for both parties. It also raises suspicions regarding the ability of either party to work well with others (Bucher and Stellings, 1977). This singular faculty-student relationship is quite different from the medical or clinical model, where multiple relationships are cultivated, or from large, part-time professional master's programs in which advising students is simply divided among advisers without concern for their particular academic interests.

Student-faculty relationships, while significant in the socialization process, differ across fields and disciplines in their frequency and intensity. Medical and law school faculty interact with students less frequently and more formally

> **The choice or assignment of a faculty adviser can be critical to the socialization process and a student's success.**

than other professions or disciplines (Becker, Geer, Hughes, and Strauss, 1961; Johnson, 1983; Epstein, 1993). Faculty often appear distant and aloof to students (Becker, Geer, Hughes, and Strauss, 1961). By contrast, informal contact among dentistry faculty and dental students helps students to grasp the role expectations of dentist and junior colleague (Platt and Branch, 1972; Quarantelli, Helfrich, and Yutsy, 1964).

Because of vastly unequal status among the partners in the student-faculty relationship, faculty may have a tendency to deal in a paternalistic manner with graduate and professional students, who are then forced to cope with a sort of "role disability." Graduate students increase their position in the student hierarchy and progress toward their professional goal with each passing year and completed examination hurdle. Yet graduate students continue to be hampered by their dependency on, and limitations with respect to, faculty in all fields as well as to clients and patients in clinical settings (Becker, Geer, Hughes, and Strauss, 1961).

Graduate students are even isolated from one another in classes and seminars in their disciplines and academic fields, thereby removing them from "outside" interference and influence. Faculty use such opportunities to determine students' investment in and commitment to their academic fields, assess the likelihood of completing the program, and determine their readiness to accept greater levels of personal and professional responsibility (Bragg, 1976). In medicine, grade pressure ensures that students learn the material. But students often feel resentment at being "forced to give up the ideal of learning for themselves in order to pass the examinations" (Becker, Geer, Hughes, and Strauss, 1961, p. 163).

Student Peer Culture

The impact of peer group members on each other generates a powerful force that nourishes and transforms members. Norris and Barnett (1994) used data from four educational administration programs that use a cohort approach (i.e., common starting date, sequencing of courses, and other requirements for members of the cohort) to learn students' perceptions of the advantages and disadvantages in terms of growth, interaction patterns, and transfer of learning. This approach is sharply different from the usual pattern of graduate work in educational administration, which is generally based on more or less willy-nilly accumulation of required courses. The data revealed that cohort groups encourage peer bonding, greater interaction, increased personal and professional growth, and group maturity. In one of several follow-up studies on cohorts that gathered data through focus groups, Norris, Basom, Barnett, and Yerkes (1996) found that the synergy generated by strong cohorts produces not only shared experiences during their time together but also starts an evolutionary growth process that extends beyond graduation and helps sustain longer-term professional development.

Graduate and professional student support groups, whether self-generated or facilitated by faculty, may provide a forum and sounding board for students to share information, anxieties, and perceptions about the department, individual faculty, classes, examinations, and job prospects. A sense of community helps graduate students to survive the anxieties and uncertainties with respect to the demands of their degree programs as well as future academic and professional role expectations (Staton and Darling, 1989).

Many arts and sciences disciplines, and educational and public administration programs, have instituted supportive, collaborative cohort environments for student entrants in addition to a traditional slate of courses. These preparation formats attempt to mirror the environment into which students will enter at the work site or in the field rather than perpetuating an isolated academic environment removed from professional practice. The belief is that academic preparation and socialization into a profession should be focused more on life after graduation and less on the academic program and the role of the graduate student (Short and Twale, 1994; Twale and Kochan, 1998, 2000).

Involvement

Deeper immersion into the graduate program comes with support systems, responsibilities, and opportunities for fulfilling expectations. The process includes learning how to think and what to believe as well as how to act in terms of assistantships, clinical experiences, and other demonstrations of pre-professional socialization supervised under the guidance of faculty and other qualified professional practitioners. While graduate students' attachments to the program, the faculty, and peers deepen, involvement stresses student loyalty and participation in the life of the profession or discipline while still under supervision and scrutiny of the faculty. Each profession or discipline differs with respect to the facilitation of involvement and expected outcomes.

Organizational Structures

Socialization varies by discipline or professional field and is influenced as well by professional boards or associations that sanction a graduate's right to practice. Bar associations and boards of specialized medical practitioners administer examinations for professional licensure in their respective fields. Clergy are recognized by divine approbation as well as by church organizational hierarchies. Educational administrators are licensed to practice through each state's educational bureaucracy, a process facilitated by higher education institutions through coursework that meets certification requirements (Daresh and Playko, 1995).

Using 148 questionnaires and forty interviews with students in arts and sciences, engineering, and social science, Slawski (1973) explored student-faculty relationships as they affected professional career development. The data showed that, in terms of the social aspect of a discipline, certain disciplines such as social sciences and humanities are more inclusive and spirited than are others such as mechanical engineering.

Socialization is affected by more frequent and varied opportunities for interaction that differ by program area or field. The socialization of neophytes tends to occur within a collective atmosphere early in the program. The socialization of doctoral ABD candidates, however, tends to be more isolated in small groups that vary with each student, thus making each experience distinct (Baird, 1990, 1992; Hill, 1973). Baird (1992) surveyed 596 University of Illinois graduate students from across disciplines and at different stages in their education to determine their relationship with faculty and their peers. He found that faculty usually report being available to graduate students, serving as mentors, and modeling research skills. Graduate programs vary, however, with respect to the levels of autonomy granted to students. Academic professionals tend to be autonomous workers, yet the ability to practice and grant autonomy varies by discipline or profession and thus is unstandardized and left to faculty discretion (Baird, 1990, 1992; Pavalko and Holley, 1974). By and large, those students afforded greater autonomy early in their career development have an advantage over those not granted autonomy until much later.

Law and medical students typically enter, progress, and graduate as a class, mainly because students tend to be full time for the entire course of their degree programs. The system, rather than the student, sets the pace. Educational administration, on the other hand, is an area where part-time students are prevalent (Twale and Kochan, 2000). A common practice with these doctoral programs is to accommodate a "stopping out" mechanism as well as part-time options, because students are older than average and tend to be employed full time. Proximity alone often dictates physical involvement in the doctoral program, but it also inadvertently affects professional involvement. In fact, part-time students are often overlooked or excluded from assistantships or funded projects because of their absence from campus.

Fields such as business and law also have part-time programs for the first professional degree (for example, M.B.A. and J.D.) that tend to be offered in the evening to students who are employed full time. The experiences of these students tend to be quite different from those of full-time students in the same fields along a number of dimensions, including access to faculty (such programs employ more part-time faculty whose primary affiliation is not with a university), interaction with peers, and opportunities for professional socialization.

Entrance into arts and sciences graduate programs has traditionally been within a year or two of undergraduate graduation, when most students have the fewest personal obligations. Immersion into the classroom and studying long hours may tend to prevent students from thinking of much else or interacting very much with each other outside the classroom (Stover, 1989). For individual students, however, the pecking order (and subsequent career sponsorship by faculty) may be determined by successful movement through formal rites of passage, periodic examinations, awards, scholarships, working with faculty on funded projects, presentation and publication of papers under faculty supervision, sole authorship of a scholarly article, and fulfilling professional and departmental service activities (Breneman, 1975; Rossman, 1995; Sheridan, 1991). Consequently, the deeper the level of involvement and the greater the student's accomplishment in the department, the greater the chance that graduate students receive strong moral and financial support from the faculty in their academic programs.

Program Structures

Students are often rated and ranked, formally or informally, by faculty. These evaluative judgments reward better students by providing various opportunities that are not open to other students (for example, access to resources for professional travel, sponsorship for special fellowships). In medical schools, for instance, students progress through formal classes as a group but as individuals in clinical settings. Faculty judgment of a student's capability of handling various situations results in a student hierarchy (Becker, Geer, Hughes, and Strauss, 1961). Students, in turn, "jockey for status and professional recognition" (Coombs, 1978, p. 256) "while simultaneously attempting to make a good impression on the faculty" (Becker, Geer, Hughes, and Strauss, 1961, p. 297).

Faculty involvement in student socialization is not always valued in the academic reward structure. Consequently, faculty may prefer to focus on their own university roles (especially research) rather than on preparing students for roles as practicing professionals. In professional programs such as education, peer interaction and alignment of students with the student peer culture tend to be even more common than faculty-student interaction. While many professional school faculty members encourage their students to participate in scholarly activities, such pursuits are rewarded in the university arena but may not be acknowledged correspondingly in applied professional settings outside academe (Stein and Weidman, 1989, 1990).

For law students, anticipatory socialization helps develop an enhanced professional self-image through simulated courtroom practice. Because law school faculty typically concentrate on academic forms of legal research and scholarship, students tend to be socialized into the more academic roles of students than into the normative expectations of future professional practice as an attorney. Faculty do serve as role models to orient students to the courtroom and the expectations of practice. They also advise students, though primarily from a faculty perspective rather than that of an actively practicing attorney (Thielens, 1980). Students acknowledge more than one reference group, however. Legal professionals are an important group with whom first year law students identify (Thielens, 1980) as "an occupational reference group" (Wallace, 1966, p. 368). As a result, the socialization process achieves closure, not upon graduation from law school or passing the bar exam, but later as the novice moves into the professional community (Thielens, 1980).

During the anticipatory stage of socialization, graduate students often enter a preprofessional curriculum holding stereotypes of their future role. Generally, faculty provide the most influential means to support or debunk such information (Quarantelli, Helfrich, and Yutsy, 1964). Using scaled instruments, Quarantelli, Helfrich, and Yutsy (1964) examined the self-image of dentists in terms of how professionalism grows from the freshman to sophomore years. These authors found that entering dental students' views of the "good dentist," including both positive and negative qualities, mirror faculty perspectives. Dental faculty proved not to be the primary influence on students' attitudes as they progress through dental school, however. In a later longitudinal study of twenty-three dental students and twenty-nine faculty using interviews and participant observation, Platt and Branch (1972) examined how students' attitudes toward professionalism compared with the faculty's attitudes over time. They discovered that significant changes in students' attitudes over the first two years of dental school were attributed to the clinical experience and patients' evaluation of their work, orientations often dissimilar from those of dental faculty.

Other professional fields try to copy the clinical approach through the practicum and internship experiences (Becker, Geer, Hughes, and Strauss, 1961). Textbook learning can consume the time of some students to the point that they neglect other aspects of their personal development, however. In fact, rather than trying to change their academic or professional environments, most graduate students tend to change themselves to fit the perceived expectations of their respective environments (Knight, 1973).

Program structures can be relaxed or rigid, thereby affecting the level of involvement. Requirements also generally become more rigorous as students' academic programs progress. For example, the dissertation phase of the Ph.D. renders many students unable to complete their doctoral programs. Graduate students who have no trouble with courses and exams in which the expectations are set by faculty can be overwhelmed by the difficulty of selecting a research topic and conceptualizing a study independently. Professional students in course-only programs such as medicine, law, or dentistry (Cahn, 1986) generally are not required to do independent research. Full-time versus part-time status in a graduate program as well as the type of research being conducted (positivistic, interpretive, qualitative, quantitative, and so on) may also prolong the student's program and make completing the dissertation within a reasonable time problematic.

For Ph.D. candidates, writing their dissertations can cause significant problems because it is not only a test of their knowledge and capacity to produce a scholarly synthesis of their comprehension but also a challenge of their ability to add something original to an existing body of knowledge. The task has neither fixed content nor time limitations, so many graduate students struggle to satisfy what may be unrealistic personal expectations. By contrast, professional licensure examinations test knowledge as well as "emotional control under duress" for prospective doctors and lawyers but are offered at fixed times with all examinees being subject to the same, well known content standards (Bledstein, 1976, p. 94).

With respect to writing the doctoral dissertation, graduate students' involvement is highly personal and extremely internalized, as the dissertation is a student's "labor of love" (or hate!). Criticism of the document by the faculty adviser tends to be taken as personalized and ego debilitating, and it may be responsible for inordinately long postponement of the completed degree. Because there is no formalized schedule for completion as there is in professional degree programs such as medicine, law, or dentistry, students determine the level of involvement and projected time frame that best fits their personal and work schedules.

Faculty Role in Supervised Practice

Many graduate programs incorporate some type of "clinical" experience in their requirements as part of the professional socialization process. This experience provides graduate students with the opportunity for professional practice under close supervision of fully qualified or licensed professionals in a relevant professional setting (for example, hospital clinic, courtroom, classroom, office, pulpit). Selection of a clinical site may be structured, calculated, and purposeful or random and haphazard, depending on its proximity to the university and the availability of supervisors. Medical interns, for example, may be extremely selective about where clinical obligations are fulfilled, as it affects further placement in residency. But part-time students (especially those in educational administration or social work and seminary students) may be less concerned with prestigious placements and more interested in proximity to home than the quality of the supervisor or the experience (Daresh and Playko, 1995).

In contrast to other graduate programs, the legal field has been criticized for limited professional socialization, namely, an education that is more effective in helping a "student learn how to think like a lawyer" (Daresh and Playko, 1995, p. 13) than to practice like one. While law students, regardless of grades, are under no obligation to seek clerkships and schools are not obliged to aid graduates with placement services, most programs provide assistance in both areas. Because passing the bar exam requires mastery of academic content and state laws rather than clerkships or internships, some law students may choose to forgo clinical experience during law school. For such students, professional socialization is quite different from that in fields requiring clinical experiences for graduation (Daresh and Playko, 1995).

For clergy, academic achievement is not necessarily predictive of the spiritual and interpersonal qualities needed to succeed in the pulpit. Field-based learning and internships with practicing clergy are necessary for students' learning and to aid in their progress toward fulfilling anticipated roles. Spiritual formation is also unique to the pastorate and largely absent from other professions and disciplines. Socialization to the clergy includes a critical reflection on one's life and how successfully one will perform the duties of a cleric (Stein, 1992). Students work with other seminarians as well as under the watchful tutelage of seminary faculty and practicing clergy (Daresh and Playko, 1995).

Holding an assistantship in the academic program also affects socialization. Once admitted to a graduate program, certain incumbents become privileged entrants into the private world of the scholar. The select few who penetrate the private domain are permitted to share that life with increasing opportunity and support for participating in research, publication, and presentations at professional meetings (Ohmann, 1990). Entry into this guarded enclave comes more easily through teaching and research assistantships, fellowships, internships, externships, and preceptorships than coursework (Breneman, 1975; Lortie, 1975).

Much research has been performed and published on the graduate assistantship (Boyd, 1989; Cardozier, 1991; Davis and Minnis, 1993; Ronkowski, 1989; Twale, Shannon, and Moore, 1997; Wilkening, 1991). Gottlieb (1961) looked at disciplines in the arts and sciences to determine whether faculty play a significant role in affecting students' career preferences for research or teaching. Myers (1995) used scaled instruments to study sixty-four graduate teaching assistants from several fields to assess students' attitudes toward communication processes and their impact on socialization into the teaching or research area. Both Gottlieb and Myers concluded that the assistantship affords a graduate student additional opportunities for socialization—both formal and informal—through contact with research and teaching faculty. Consequently, faculty should seriously consider their roles as models and supervisors to new graduate student assistants as well as their responsibility for the professional growth and development of advisees.

Faculty occupy an auspicious position because graduate assistants are in a position to observe, emulate, and incorporate both the positive and the negative aspects of what faculty do (Sprague and Nyquist, 1989). Faculty contributions to student development change as the graduate assistant grows into increasingly more responsible roles (Sprague and Nyquist, 1989). Faculty also are primary influences on students' intellectual, socioemotional, and occupational identity (Kirk and Todd-Mancillas, 1991). Faculty have the opportunity to help build students' self-efficacy when they offer graduate students opportunities to test and hone a variety of skills (Mann, 1994). Shannon, Twale, and Moore (1998), surveying 129 graduate teaching assistants across departments in a research university, studied the effects of training and teaching experience on students' evaluations of teaching as compared with self-ratings. Although self-ratings of the graduate teaching assistants were higher than their students' ratings, faculty were involved in only minimal efforts to train and socialize graduate students for their teaching role, thus perpetuating a culture of limited attention to course instruction.

Attraction to research interests affects the department's and university's social capital in that good faculty tend to attract high-quality students who, in turn, attract better, more productive faculty (LaPidus, 1977). In the process, however, those graduate students placed in teaching assistantships may be doubly shortchanged in their graduate experience. Even though teaching assistants should be involved in a true apprenticeship under continued guidance and support from a master teacher known for superior teaching (Wilkening, 1991), faculty in research institutions may tend to slight teaching in favor of research, leaving them little time to serve as mentors to their graduate assistants in the area of teaching (Cardozier, 1991). Further, graduate teaching assistants, while doing important work of the academic program, are not as involved in research that may lead to publication and strengthening their bargaining position in the academic labor market.

Greater peer interaction among graduate teaching assistants affects their socialization into the teaching profession (Jones, 1991). The socialization process can be exceptionally rewarding or woefully lacking, however. There is little doubt that those graduate students holding assistantships are more likely to experience greater faculty contact and collegiality than their peers without assistantships (Breneman, 1975; Sheridan, 1991). In fact, the status differential that exists between the research and the teaching assistantship affects the quality of the graduate experience. The best and brightest graduate students are usually recruited into research assistantships and fellowships, while the rest are given teaching assignments (Sullivan, 1991).

Teaching assistants tend to have more contact with other teaching assistants, while research assistants usually have more interaction with faculty and work more in isolation from other students (Brown, 1970). This practice conveys the message that research takes precedence over teaching and is supported by a policy and reward system upheld by faculty at research institutions (Cardozier, 1991). For example, if faculty are perceived by their doctoral students as interested in research, faculty tend to guide students toward a preference for research over teaching, and the students will be better prepared for an academic position, having followed this guiding hand (Gottlieb, 1961).

Graduate teaching assistants are often afforded little advance notice of the class to be covered; given short-term, hurried, generic, or no advanced training;

and receive poor long-term supervision or feedback (Boyd, 1989; Davis and Minnis, 1993). Ronkowski and Iannaccone (1989) surveyed 224 graduate teaching assistants across departments on teaching concerns, focusing on whether these teaching assistants perceived the learning environment for teaching assistants to be developmental. Respondents indicated that, as teaching assistants, they tended to learn from on-the-job training, primarily trial and error aided by feedback from students' evaluations of teaching. Bomotti (1994) questioned eighty-six graduate teaching assistants in the arts and sciences. Using factor analysis and discriminate analysis to identify which factors determined whether teaching assistants pursued or abandoned academic careers and which factors particularly influenced their career path, she learned that a graduate student's teaching career may be influenced more by good faculty supervision during graduate school, in general, than just the teaching experience alone. Faculty members' relationships with graduate teaching assistants affect identification with the department in terms of students' willingness to pattern their classroom behavior and teaching style after a respected professor (Jones, 1991). While research assistants appear to be gaining the necessary socialization into academic careers in those institutions in which research is highly valued, teaching assistants do not always benefit from comparable opportunities for professional development (Anderson, 1996; Boyd, 1989; Davis and Minnis, 1993).

Graduate assistantships can also provide a mechanism for faculty control and regulation of students' actions (Staton and Darling, 1989). Historically, the norm has been that the graduate student "acknowledges the authority" of the faculty mentor and subjugates herself or himself "in all matters relevant to the socialization process" in exchange for departmental faculty validation of competence at graduation and sponsorship in applications for professional positions (Rosen and Bates, 1967, p. 80). This type of paternalistic mentality, in the absence of nurturing and support, might well hinder development of truly independent and creative scholars.

Expected Outcomes

Opportunities to gain entry to a profession by first being colleagues-in-training (assistantships, fellowships, preceptorships) offer the student the prospect of developing confidence, insight, and professional identity. These types of positions provide opportunities for graduate students to demonstrate knowledge, skills, and competence while moving into the professional realm (Sprague and Nyquist, 1989) and to be supported both emotionally and financially (Kirk and Todd-Mancillas, 1991).

The degree of autonomy given by the faculty and the amount of independence exhibited by the graduate student are critical to the faculty-student relationship. The relationship with an adviser depends on the extent to which graduate students are supported in their career development and their more personal needs, particularly through interactive rapport. The socialization process provides more effective facilitation of attaining desired professional goals when both areas are fulfilled (Hockin, 1981). Socialization of graduate students into the academic program is facilitated through communication and active learning as well as social and emotional support systems, so that graduate students acquire necessary information in policy, teaching, and research as well as participate actively in the life of the academic program (Breneman, 1975; Kirk and Todd-Mancillas, 1991; Sheridan, 1991; Staton and Darling, 1989).

> **The degree of autonomy given by the faculty and the amount of independence exhibited by the graduate student are critical to the faculty-student relationship.**

Faculty in the physical and biological sciences emphasize training graduate students to be researchers, while humanities faculty prepare both teachers and scholars. Natural science disciplines provide greater research supervision by faculty than other disciplines, thus enhancing students' socialization into research-oriented careers and universities. Social science departments train researchers and teachers about equally. The master's and doctoral level professions train for advanced career pursuits (LaPidus, 1977). Time to complete a degree is longer for humanities and social science students and shorter for the sciences and medical fields. Most doctoral degree programs in education are designed to accommodate part-time students and therefore tend to offer programs that take longer to complete.

Kyvik and Smeby (1994), studying faculty in multidisciplinary areas in Norway, used a questionnaire to assess the degree to which research faculty involve students in their projects. Results showed that the natural sciences and medical fields create a dependency on faculty among students but that graduate students are more likely to work with faculty on research projects. In the case of the natural sciences, faculty advisers often identify dissertation topics and secure the resources to complete the research in a timely fashion because it is an integral part of the faculty members' ongoing research programs. In contrast, faculty in the humanities and social sciences do not do as much joint collaboration and publishing with students, a factor that adversely affects the socialization of these students, who may also experience more difficulty in selecting a dissertation topic, staying on task, and finishing doctoral degrees in a timely fashion.

The curricular process through which medical students pass over the course of four years is more deliberate and prescribed than that found in the arts and sciences. Medical school also operates as a closed system, encompassing and engrossing students in the knowledge, as well as the life, of their chosen profession of medicine. Correspondingly, as these students proceed toward their goal of becoming physicians, they grow more homogeneous. Students share competition, conflict, cooperation, and unity. This experience helps medical students experience and imitate as well as interpret their environment (Becker, Geer, Hughes, and Strauss, 1961; Coombs, 1978; Hafferty and Franks, 1994; Weinholtz, 1991).

While all students deal with the stress of examinations and assignments, nowhere is it more compelling than in the medical curriculum (Coombs, 1978). The socialization process for medical students includes not only the science of medicine but also learning to deal with intimate issues, chronic and terminal illness, and death as part of their intensive clinical experience. The clinical experience set in the organizational structure of the hospital forces students to assimilate new perspectives not amenable to traditional classroom settings (Becker, Geer, Hughes, and Strauss, 1961). Social distance between student and clinician is far less than that between student and academic faculty; the converse is true, however, for doctoral students in the disciplines and professions (Coombs, 1978).

Students' Involvement With Peers

Peers can be both competitive and cooperative, aiding as well as hindering one another in graduate and professional programs. While cooperation can happen informally, much has been written about the formal use of cohorts in the training and socialization of neophytes. Cohort programs can offer social outlets, psychological release, and much needed emotional support. Members of cohorts serve as professional networks and information sources as well as verbal handbooks that supply fellow classmates with informal departmental and university standards and practice. They can become assignment clarifiers, reality checkers, surrogate families, sounding boards, and progress monitors. Through the established cohort, isolation can be reduced for students who hold assistantships or study primarily under one faculty member. Cohorts offer much needed consolation to the part-time student, who rarely experiences the university beyond scheduled classes (Basom, Yerkes, Norris, and Barnett, 1996; Twale and Kochan, 1998). In addition, graduate student cohorts can flourish with a mix of gender, exceptionality, ethnicity, color, age, personality, and perspective.

> **[Peers] can become assignment clarifiers, reality checkers, surrogate families, sounding boards, and progress monitors.**

Twale and Kochan (1998) surveyed fifty-one educational administration students and conducted focus groups to determine the benefits of cohorts in successive years for part-time students in a fourteen-month doctoral seminar. While the seminar format promoted the attributes of peer interaction and collaborative community, the ability to sustain community following the seminar was greatly diminished for these part-timers. Because student peers in educational administration, for instance, may be practicing professionals drawn from multiple areas, peer groups offer the emotional and professional support important for students' success beyond the university department (Stein and Weidman, 1989, 1990).

Peer and cohort groups in psychiatry have been noted as important to students' success. Information on supervisors is likely to be exchanged along with theoretical and factual material, therapeutic remedies, scholarly work, and patient information. In contrast, biochemistry students tend not to develop strong peer group attachments that allow for information exchange (Bucher and Stellings, 1977).

Among medical students, a sense of shared struggle bonds peers together. Teamwork in the clinical phase of socialization is manifest during attending rounds (Weinholtz, 1991). In fact, students are more likely to find comfort and solace in their common struggle during their internships and residencies than with faculty in medical school or physicians in rounds (Weinholtz, 1991). Ironically, team learning and bonding through medical school and rounds vanishes after graduation when the new physician enters a solitary professional practice. The role becomes more competitive as the doctor climbs a hierarchy, collaborates with and has status over certain other health care professionals, yet remains in a subordinate role to senior physicians in the clinical setting (Weinholtz, 1991).

Peer group culture and cohort solidarity wane in most fields of graduate and professional study as students progress through their programs. This gravitational pull of students toward selected faculty and away from other students and faculty less interested in a particular research topic or subspecialty affects graduate students' socialization and subsequent professional development (Hockin, 1981). As peer group members mature professionally and move in different directions, the group established in graduate school gradually fragments to permit students' integration into the professional realm (Twale and Kochan, 1998). Likewise, as students in the medical fields are given the opportunity to view both the clinical setting and the faculty practicing medicine, students shift their identification from classroom to professional practice (Caplovitz, 1980). In the arts and sciences, as faculty and students draw closer together for the research and dissertation phase, graduate students begin to experience the professional isolation associated with the faculty role in academe to which many aspire upon graduation (Hockin, 1981).

Structural Engagement

Commitment comes through bonding processes with peers and faculty, the sponsorship of a mentor, and internalization of the professional role. Culmination of the student role occurs as the steps necessary for assuming full responsibility in professional roles (i.e., board exams, licensure, credentialing, dissertation defense, and employment in the field of training) are taken. Identification with professional roles, professional practice, and advancing academic disciplines affirms professional competence and commitment.

Forming Collaborative Bonds

Whether among peers or with faculty, collaboration is a means to share knowledge with others in order to expand horizons. Working with others in the university setting and extending into the professional community promote closer affiliation with one's chosen field. Anderson (1996) looked at more than eleven hundred doctoral students in research universities from the hard sciences, civil engineering, and the social sciences, and assessed the level of collaborative activity and faculty guidance as it related to students' socialization into academe and the life of the mind. The data showed that this bond strengthens as the student reaches professional status and continues the collaborative process. Highly participatory settings encourage a better environment in which to study, especially in the arts and sciences, to hone research skills necessary for doctoral students who seek the research professoriat. Collaboration in research is more prevalent for the hard than for the soft sciences, however (Anderson, 1996). Collaboration in one's graduate academic program supports sound research models of coauthoring, entrenchment in interdepartmental activities, and a better sense of inclusiveness with, rather than isolation from, faculty and peers (Anderson, 1996).

Collaborative efforts often lead to research presentations and articles in scholarly journals. In turn, journal acceptance means the beginning of professional acceptance and recognition. Failure to make professional presentations and to publish one's research and scholarship results in lack of professional recognition in one's academic field (Brown, 1970). Thus, cohesiveness through collaboration forms a research community that increases the cultural capital of its members, both faculty and graduate students and assists faculty in "instilling work discipline and achievement values in their [students]" (Portes and MacLeod, 1996, p. 257). Of course, collaboration may conflict with norms for promotion and tenure in many research universities that give more weight to single-author than coauthored publications.

Demonstrating Competence and Level of Commitment

Educational processes and expectations differ across professional and disciplinary programs (Olmsted and Paget, 1969). For instance, while all graduate and professional students must demonstrate competence before faculty, medical students must also demonstrate competence before patients and their families (Coombs, 1978). Ironically, even those medical students who are well versed in scientific knowledge may manifest a poor bedside manner (Coombs, 1978). "Since medical education does not emphasize doctor/patient communication, over time students may place less importance on giving information to patients concerning diagnosis and treatment as they get caught up in learning the more technical aspects of medicine" (Leserman, 1981, p. 28).

Commitment versus credentialism also separates professional fields and university disciplines. In most cases, lawyers, doctors, and clergy have a high level of commitment to their profession and a long period of induction and practice. Educational administrators, by contrast, can obtain credentials at various points in their career, usually by attending a part-time graduate program. Further, they may not necessarily become a school principal or superintendent immediately upon graduation. Incumbents to the administrator role may experience no period of induction comparable to other professional fields. The opportunity to feel like a doctor, lawyer, or member of the clergy as a result of an intense learning and socialization process is key. For educational administrators, however, the need to feel like a practicing administrator seems to be far less intense (Daresh and Playko, 1995; Stein and Weidman, 1989, 1990).

Because comprehensive exams for academic and professional doctorates tend to be scheduled when students decide they are ready, graduate students may tend to feel isolated in preparing for them and in trying to develop a dissertation topic independently. Some students find support in peer- or faculty-led student groups, but others lose interest entirely and never complete a doctoral dissertation.

With respect to socialization into the field of social work, newly entering graduate students need not possess the bachelor's degree in social work, because the graduate curriculum and practicum or fieldwork help them through the socialization process. Induction into the social work profession may require graduate students to shift existing belief systems, a form of resocialization. Surveying seventy master's degree students in social work, Manzo and Ross-Gordon (1990) sought to determine the inclination of these students to internalize professional social work values as they progressed through their graduate degree programs. The authors found that most graduate students must change their thinking before the socialization process can begin. Yet immersion into the professional culture or prolonged exposure to it does not guarantee that graduates will hold the traditional values of the social work profession (Ketefian, 1993).

Moreover, in some professional areas such as public administration, students often exhibit naivete by neglecting to interact with practitioners in their field, thinking that affiliation alone will make them successful. The key to professional success often comes initially through demonstrating academic mastery of the theoretical frameworks of the profession. In the field, the world of academe is physically separated from the professional community. While faculty are able to include practitioners in classroom discussion, separation from public administrators can hinder their ability to step into the public arena and thus carry their students with them. Fieldwork projects and internships, however, help to bridge that gap (Nalbandian, 1980).

In a recent longitudinal study, Olsen and Crawford (1998) studied fifty-four junior faculty from across departments at a research institution using semistructured interviews, questionnaires, and institutional documents. They found that "graduate program preparation provided anticipatory information of faculty role and professional norms, values, and expectations, and that preparation gave way to on-the-job learning" by "balancing demands, setting priorities, and establishing collegial relations" (p. 51).

Using semistructured interviews of thirty-one senior research faculty specializing in the higher educational administration curriculum across the country, Creamer and McGuire (1998) found "cumulative advantage" to be the key to productivity after receiving the degree. Earning a doctorate, especially for the women in the study, did not necessarily prepare the recipient to publish as a junior faculty member. Regardless of gender, however, publication productivity was enhanced by continued interaction with the graduate school faculty mentor or collegial networks of collaborating peers who supported and critiqued each other's work.

From knowledge acquisition to primary investment to increased involvement, socialization of graduate students takes on varying forms so that students reach the required levels of personal and professional competence as well as commitment to a particular field or profession. While a formal, highly structured socialization process may produce the desired result in some disciplines and professions, others accomplish similar results in less formal ways. The approaches affect students differently, especially underrepresented groups new to academe. Exposing differences sets the stage for reflecting not only on how we socialize and prepare professionals but also on how this socialization and preparation can be done more effectively and less intrusively in ways that are more sensitive to increasingly diverse groups of graduate students. Knowledge of a range of disciplinary and professional areas broadens our base for improving the processes now in use while still preserving the distinctiveness and integrity of the programs needed to educate future professionals.

Table 3 highlights representative characteristics of socialization by structural element in the specific professional or academic areas to which they apply. Similarly constructed, Table 4 highlights representative outcomes of socialization by structural elements, also by profession or disciplinary grouping. Taken together, these tables provide a synopsis of the key issues discussed in this section. The final section addresses some of the ways the stress and discontinuities in socializing graduate students can be eased and suggests strategies for modifying and improving graduate degree programs.

TABLE 3
Representative Characteristics of Socialization by Graduate Academic Field

Structural Element	Profession: Law, Medicine, Dentistry	Master's and Doctoral Professions	Arts and Sciences Disciplines
Department, Program, Discipline	Tightly configured, serial socialization, specialized.	Loosely configured, disjunctive socialization, independent thought.	Classified. disjunctive socialization, independent scholarship.
Faculty Functions	Sort and select by entrance exams, academic achievement; role is formal, distant, prescribed; student accepts authority.	Sort and select by recommendation, calling, personal choice, exams; role is less formal and more advisory; relationships vary.	Sort and select by entrance exams and rigorous standards, role is less formal and more advisory; relationships vary.
Curriculum	Highly prescribed, based on acquisition of skills, clinical rounds.	Less highly prescribed; immersion based on professional practice; practica, internships; problem-based learning.	Immersion into the discipline and academe, research model.
Student Autonomy	Minimal, few if any assistantships.	Some guidance and supervision, few assistantships.	Mostly assistantships, supervised as research assistant, unsupervised as teaching assistant.
Student Peer Culture	Teams, study groups.	Informal groupings, part-time cohort groups.	Formal full-time cohorts.
Professionalization	Need for role models outside academe, skill competency, clinical competency.	Role models and mentors on site, professional competency.	Role models and mentors in academe, academic rigor, meet faculty standards.

TABLE 4

Representative Outcomes of Socialization by Graduate Academic Field

Structural Element	Professions: Law, Medicine, Dentistry	Master's and Doctoral Professions	Arts and Sciences Disciplines
Department, Program, Discipline	Professional role learning, clinical competence, right to practice with license.	Professional role learning; practical competence; certification, licensure, ordination.	Academic role learning, research competence, academic faculty or research associate position.
Faculty Functions	Emulation by students, conformity, role internalization.	Practical collaboration, professional entry, networking.	Supervising collaboration, academic entry gatekeepers, validation of ability.
Curriculum	Designed to pass boards.	Perform field experience, professional development, practical experience.	Theory building, research design and interpretation.
Student Autonomy	Private practice, consulting.	Supervisory role, collaborative community, congregation, administrative decision making.	Academic role, isolation, collegiality, research projects.
Student Peer Culture	Professional colleagues.	Team, networking, collaborative community, support system.	Research collaborators.
Professionalization	Commitment to profession, personal lifestyle, licensure.	Thesis/dissertation defense, certification, ordination, licensure.	Dissertation defense, faculty appointment, research associate, postdoctoral work, publications, presentations.

Easing the Perilous Passage

REDUCING THE STRESS encountered by graduate students as they progress through the perilous passage toward a graduate degree would ideally begin with systemic change, but modifying academic programs is a reasonable alternative and a good first step. Faculty should find ways to increase diversity, offer both financial and moral support, and modify their own behavior when necessary. This final section suggests some ways in which these areas can be addressed and some directions for the future.

Modifying the Program

The literature on socialization reviewed in previous sections spans the 1950s through the 1990s. Few substantive changes in the preparation of professionals or academics have succeeded in revolutionizing the socialization process. Instead, methods passed from generation to generation, however archaic or flawed, have remained in vogue. Whether neophytes are socialized primarily for studenthood or for the professional roles to which they aspire remains unclear. Should professional socialization begin during graduate school or should it wait until after students move into full professional roles? Or should the process be a seamless, continuous one that begins with anticipatory socialization before graduate

> **Few substantive changes in the preparation of professionals or academics have succeeded in revolutionizing the socialization process.**

school and is then built on through role performance, experiential activities, and professional development?

To illustrate, clergy heed a calling while nurtured within a religious environment. This calling is then followed by entrance into a theological program that provides academic content and therefore secular legitimization for that calling. On the other hand, law students are socialized as students, not as lawyers. To discover that the courtroom is markedly different from the classroom may cause disillusionment for some graduates. Therefore, throughout their three-year program, law students could benefit from more exposure to the legal world they have chosen to enter, realistic mentoring, and mandated clerkships. Theological students, having already developed a professional awareness through their faith and exposure to a religious environment, must match while in seminary how their faith and previous knowledge fit with the theoretical and historical content of classroom material.

Focusing on graduate and professional school expectations or outcomes may require a reexamination of the socialization process, because students, to graduate and eventually succeed in their fields, need to be prepared for all aspects of the student role as well as prospective professional roles (Daresh and Playko, 1995). As a result, although cosmetic changes in program structure may be the easiest to accomplish, a total program evaluation and subsequent makeover may prove more beneficial in the long run (Senge, 1990). In preparing educational leaders, for example, Scheurich and Laible (1995) recommend "a major transformation, a major realignment of our entire way of preparing educational administrators" (p. 319). In fact, workforce preparation has shifted away from glorifying isolated specialties to encouraging cooperative, diverse, collaborative teams that contribute to the overall group (Geltner, 1994), regardless of discipline or profession.

Coincidently, general information about the concept of learning organizations has penetrated the literature of the 1990s. Senge (1990) has been a major proponent of this challenging, supportive type of environment, even though academe has traditionally fostered isolation among faculty, a reality often noted in student/faculty pairings during the dissertation phase of doctoral study. Likewise, Senge's learning organizations (1990), Helgesen's web of inclusion (1995), and de Geus's living community (1997) offer similar alternative approaches to academe, all of which champion ecological changes that could bridge isolation and encourage team learning, mutual sharing, bonding, interaction, tolerance, group maturity, cohesiveness, collaborative community, and diminished power structures.

More collaborative, holistic approaches to learning necessitate systemic change that challenges most existing approaches to graduate and professional study (Basom, Yerkes, Norris, and Barnett, 1996; Moller, 1998; Norris and Barnett, 1994). Many graduate programs still maintain the use of committees for examinations and dissertation phases, yet committees rarely function as interactive, power neutral teams. The traditional omnipresent superordinate/subordinate power differentials in academe contradict the notion that learning organizations should be noncoercive. Quite promising along these lines is the participative and cooperative engagement approach to program development advocated by Haworth and Conrad (1997).

Increasing Diversity

A study of midwestern colleges and universities identified twenty-six exemplary programs for increasing the representation of faculty of color (Turner, Myers, and Creswell, 1999). The characteristics of these programs are also quite common in university programs for increasing representation and retention of graduate students of color, namely, "fellowships, special hiring programs or contracts, and mentoring and networking opportunities" (Turner, Myers, and Creswell, 1999, p. 47). These types of exemplary programs were, however, also found to have three significant constraints: "(a) many are fully or partially funded on 'soft monies'; (b) due in part to inadequate funding, little or no formative or summative evaluations are conducted of cost and effectiveness; and (c) such programs are, in the main, not systemic but isolated attempts by a department or a special program within the college" (p. 47).

The researchers concluded that institutions must develop more welcoming climates for faculty of color, celebrating and welcoming diversity on their campuses through the creation of a culture of pluralism: "we argue that what unifies us is a common attention to, and respect for, dependence on, and appreciation of our differences. When we share a culture that values our diversity, we all have a stake in maintaining that culture. Conversely, an emphasis on sameness (for example, conformity to dominant cultural norms) marginalizes and alienates those who feel different or are perceived as different. Inclusiveness leads to unity; conformity leads to division" (Turner, Myers, and Creswell, 1999, p. 54).

Consumers increasingly demand more from professionals. And professionals must, in turn, deal with an increasingly diverse clientele. These trends alone should call into question certain aspects of graduate and professional training. "Because this is the way it has always been done" no longer suffices as a reason for maintaining the status quo. Welcoming a diversity of neophytes into a graduate or professional program means addressing cultural issues, acknowledging varying learning styles, modifying interactive patterns, acknowledging physical limitations, and providing emotional security for graduate students who speak in new and different voices. These areas challenge faculty to reconfigure existing programs to be more inclusive.

Developing greater flexibility and more options for students so that graduates are more versatile, attracting more women and minority group members, and providing better information about careers continue to be among the major areas of improvement advocated by major national commissions (Committee on Science, Engineering, and Public Policy, 1995). Modifications and adaptive strategies on the part of programs and students are necessary. The newer approaches to teaching and learning embrace collaborative, cooperative, and reflective strategies that bring together graduate students, faculty, and practitioners in a more communicative, heterarchical environment (Barr and Tagg, 1995). Conceivably, the use of more cooperative strategies would also soften the competitive nature of some graduate programs.

Offering Support for Students

Graduate student clienteles have changed more than have the programs that attract them. Affirmative action and targeted recruitment have increased the diversity of entering classes of students, but universal means of addressing support and retention of all students progressing through graduate and professional programs remain sporadic (Twale, Douvanis, and Sekula, 1992). Entrance rates continue to be higher than graduation rates, which in turn provides the ripple effect of shrinking the number of professionals in the field who can serve as role models for future entering classes (Turner, Myers, and Creswell, 1999).

Whether the support is financial, tutorial, social, or emotional, the needs of all students must be considered in the socialization and professionalization process. For example, while some professional programs naturally put students in groups or teams, other programs in the disciplines socialize students in a more isolated, individualistic manner. Some students may *need* individual attention, however, while isolated individuals may benefit from working on collaborative projects with other students and faculty as well as working with their major professor (Golde, 2000).

Too often students are trained in serial fashion to fit rigid normative expectations. Faculty and practitioners might consider creating interactive environments that encourage students to take risks, to think independently and outside the box, and to reflect critically on thought and action. Graduate and professional programs need to move away from training students to fit the status quo and toward socializing them to challenge and improve their chosen profession and its concomitant process of professionalization.

Too often students are trained in serial fashion to fit rigid normative expectations.

Collaborative communities offer opportunities for students' self-reflection; they also enhance tolerance, appreciation, and understanding for each other. Cockrell, Caplow, and Donaldson (2000, p. 360) regard collaborative groups as promoting discourse that "enculturates students into communities of practice and develops ownership of knowledge linked to the language of the discipline." When students learn to function collaboratively in their graduate program, they can more easily sustain membership in collaborative environments as they move out of their student roles and into their professional roles (Twale, Kochan, and Reed, 1999, 2000). Mutual support helps these students express their commonalities and differences as they make sense of their individual and collective experiences (Newman, 1994; Welton, 1993).

Establishing significant mentoring opportunities is an approach that has been advocated consistently as a way to facilitate the personal and professional development of graduate students with diverse characteristics across the spectrum of fields (Willie, Grady, and Hope, 1991; Blackwell, 1987; Turner, Myers, and Creswell, 1999; Committee on Science, Engineering, and Public Policy, 1997). A comprehensive socialization strategy should include mentoring of new graduate students by more advanced students and faculty mentoring of all graduate students in their academic degree programs.

By examining current professional and graduate programs across phases of students' socialization into the profession, similarities and differences become apparent. Strengths and weaknesses are defined and may be evaluated. Because graduate students value the importance of community through cohort and other collaborative experiences (Golde, 2000), socialization of graduate and professional students should be thought of as a process of mutual exchange rather than as something done to students by faculty. By being immersed in a collaborative community, students and faculty can consciously and conscientiously help sustain that community, so that support, protection during experimentation and risk taking, and emotional security are encouraged.

> **Socialization of graduate and professional students should be thought of as a process of mutual exchange rather than as something done to students by faculty.**

While Moller (1998) asserted that "leaders need a safe environment for personal and professional renewal" (p. 48), Twale and Kochan (2000) found in their study of cohorts in graduate educational leadership programs that participants, especially women and people of color, did not always perceive the environment as being safe enough to take risks. With more diverse students and increased numbers of part-time students and distance learning programs, physical, proximal, professional, and psychological bonding become challenging, not only during formally structured academic programs but especially when classes end. Graduate programs will have not only to create more supportive and collaborative environments in the face of increasing diversity but also to sustain them over time.

Collaborative learning communities, while helpful for many different types of graduate students, seem to be especially critical for the growing population of part-time and distance learning students. Alternative formats to the traditional cohort model have been attempted that encompass both the academic and social aspects critical to persistence and successful professional socialization. Exploratory study has uncovered attempts to create community through group assignments, field experiences, e-mail, listservs, chat rooms, bulletin boards, mentoring, networking, joint publication and presentation, and numerous social events (Anderson and Garrison, 1998; Porter, 1997; Twale, Kochan, and Reed, 2000).

Several excellent resources provide assessments of the graduate school experience and examples of approaches that have been developed to facilitate the passage of graduate students through their degree programs.[1] Anderson's volume (1998) covers a variety of topics, including the graduate student experience, best practices for students' enculturation, attrition of first-year doctoral students, and "survival skills." Another volume in the same series addresses the dissertation process (Goodchild, Green, Katz, and Kluever, 1997). Finally, a monograph edited by Pruitt-Logan and Isaac (1995) describes a variety of important services often needed by graduate students, including personal and career counseling, financial aid, and housing. This volume also provides suggestions for dealing with needs of graduate students from diverse cultures and

---

[1] Several particularly interesting and informative Web sites provide resources for prospective academics, current faculty, and graduate program administrators that also address issues in the socialization of graduate and professional students. See, for example, (1) "Tomorrow's Professor Listserv" (http://sll.stanford.edu/projects/tomprof/), managed by the Stanford University Learning Laboratory; (2) "Preparing Future Faculty . . . a national network of academic leaders reshaping graduate education to include preparation for the full range of faculty roles subsumed by the terms teaching, research, and service" (http://www.preparing-faculty.org), a collaborative effort of the Association of American Colleges and Universities and the Council of Graduates sponsored by The Pew Charitable Trusts and the National Science Foundation; (3) "Diversityweb" (http://www.diversityweb.org), a joint project of the University of Maryland and the Association of American Colleges and Universities supported with funds from the Ford Foundation that includes, among other things, syllabi and resources for faculty development and transformation across the disciplines; (4) Council of Graduate Schools (http://www.cgsnet.org), which contains a variety of sources related to graduate education, including on-line copies of its monthly publication, *Communicator.*

backgrounds, including foreign nationals, students of color, students with disabilities, and gay, lesbian, bisexual, and transgender students.

Modifying Faculty and Administrative Roles

Faculty and practicing professionals have served a gatekeeping function, upholding the mystique that pervades entry into professions. Holding auspicious positions has not always been in the best interest of the student or the professional field. Therefore, faculty may need to reexamine their role as gatekeepers and minimize any paternalistic tendencies they may harbor that prevent students from developing fully into their professional role. Independent thinking and progress toward the goal of professional entry should be celebrated and encouraged, not hampered through poor faculty advising or preoccupation with other aspects of the faculty role.

As much as faculty and practitioners should determine when a student is ready to fill the professional role, graduate students should have already developed their own internal mechanisms that also determine when they are ready to enter the professional ranks. Lincoln (2000) advocates a move away from the centuries-old "graduate school" to a shared, caring, reciprocal "learning community." A great love for learning should be shared with colleagues and graduate students. The community should be participatory, engaging, reflective, and critical if students are to see knowledge beyond faculty content and develop their own perspectives and original thoughts. Put otherwise, the relationship of faculty to students, or practitioner to students, should be interactive, collaborative, open, and mutually evaluative. Relationships need not be power based but should be more interactive, with faculty-student, teaching, and research relationships more cooperative.

The relationship of faculty to students, or practitioner to students, should be interactive, collaborative, open, and mutually evaluative.

The graduate teaching assistantship represents a significant preprofessional area where not enough faculty involvement, encouragement, mentoring, and monitoring have occurred. Marincovich, Prostko, and Stout (1998) are the editors of an excellent resource on the professional development of graduate teaching assistants. Faculty members can be encouraged to take advantage of resources that are available to assist with the development of mentoring skills (see, for example, Committee on Science, Engineering, and Public Policy, 1997; University of Michigan, Rackham Graduate School, 2000a, 2000b). Regardless of the field, each area calls for more professional development for faculty, students, and practitioners so they remain responsive to the ever changing dynamics involved in the socialization process, whether disciplinary, demographic, or technological. Professional development activities should also offer insights and strategies for demystifying professions and their socialization processes.

One concern echoed by faculty is the feeling of isolation, either physically or socially, of one discipline from another or by specialties within a discipline or field. Add to this feeling competition for scarce resources, publications in prestigious journals, and tenure track positions in research institutions, and even the most intellectually stimulating professions have the potential for including many lonely and isolated individuals. The notion of collaborative community and the variety of technological possibilities, however, can alter academe in ways that help bridge the isolation of faculty, professionals, and students (Muse, 1999).

Advances that have enhanced instructional delivery and aided social communication and professional collaboration (Privateer, 1999) should be incorporated effectively into graduate preparation programs. Approaches emphasizing more faculty-student interaction and collaboration may be more effective than models that foster competitiveness and professorial power. Because many of the issues carry over to graduate school, much can be learned from research on the socialization and career progress of faculty about what can be done to improve the lot of graduate students who go into academic careers (Tierney and Rhoads, 1994; Tierney and Bensimon, 1996; Turner, Myers, and Creswell, 1999).

Institutions can take active steps that have been advocated to support women in graduate programs but are also applicable to all graduate students:

1. Monitoring admissions for fairness and equity;
2. Providing realistic and informative orientations to graduate study;

3. Fostering a collegial learning environment;
4. Developing transparent rules and procedures, including examinations;
5. Countering isolation and fostering integration;
6. Providing workshops on such topics as sexual harassment, diversity, and ethics; and
7. Improving graduate student services (Nerad and Cerny, 1999, pp. 4–5).

Finally, it is incumbent upon faculty, administrators, and practicing professionals to socialize for expectations and outcomes that imply a seamless, continuous process from studenthood into desired professional roles (in both academic and nonacademic settings) yet one that also feeds back into itself for improving quality. The ongoing interaction of faculty, administrator, student, and professional serves as an adjustment mechanism in response to the changing requirements of a dynamic environment. Such interaction also encourages professionals, faculty, administrators, and students to continually reexamine process and product to determine whether modification is needed.

More important, the process of graduate and professional socialization is dynamic, not static, and it should reflect changing global trends, technology, diverse populations, and societal demands for educating skilled professionals. A reflective, interactive approach opens the door for true collaboration, sharing, and growth to promote healthy relationships that can strengthen professionalism and restructure the process of professionalization. Perhaps there is no true ending befitting an analysis of graduate and professional student socialization, because the work should reflect a journey that has no ending, only many exciting and beneficial beginnings.

References

Anderson, M. S. (1996). Collaboration, the doctoral experience, and the departmental environment. *Review of Higher Education, 19*(3), 305–326.

Anderson, M. S. (Ed.). (1998). *The experience of being in graduate school: An exploration.* New Directions for Higher Education, no. 101. San Francisco: Jossey-Bass.

Anderson, T., and Garrison, D. (1998). Learning in higher education. In C. C. Gibson (Ed.), *Distance learning in higher education* (pp. 97–112). Madison, WI: Atwood.

Antony, J. S. (forthcoming). Reexamining doctoral student socialization and professional development: Moving beyond the congruence and assimilation orientation. In J. C. Smart (Ed.), *Higher education: Handbook of theory and research* (Vol. 17). New York: Agathon.

Arnett, J. J. (2000). Emerging adulthood: A theory of development from the late teens through the twenties. *American Psychologist, 55*(5), 469–480.

Astin, A. (1984). Student involvement: A developmental theory for higher education. *Journal of College Student Personnel, 25*(4), 297–308.

Baird, L. L. (1990). The melancholy of anatomy: The personal and professional development of graduate and professional students. In J. C. Smart (Ed.), *Higher education: Handbook of theory and research* (Vol. 6, pp. 361–392). New York: Agathon.

Baird, L. L. (1992). *The stages of the doctoral career: Socialization and its consequences.* Paper presented at the annual meeting of the American Educational Research Association, San Francisco. (ED 348 925)

Barr, R., and Tagg, J. (1995). Teaching to learning: A new paradigm for undergraduate education. *Change, 27*(6), 12–25.

Basom, M., Yerkes, D., Norris, C., and Barnett, B. (1996). Using cohorts as a means for developing transformational leaders. *Journal of School Leadership, 6*(1), 99–112.

Bean, J. (1998). Alternative models of professional roles: New languages to reimagine faculty work. *Journal of Higher Education, 69*(5), 496–512.

Becker, H. S., and Carper, J. (1956a). The development of identification with an occupation. *American Journal of Sociology, 61*(4), 289–298.

Becker, H. S., and Carper, J. (1956b). The elements of identification with an occupation. *American Sociological Review, 21*(3), 341–348.

Becker, H. S., Geer, B., Hughes, E. C., and Strauss, A. (1961). *Boys in white: Student culture in medical school.* Chicago: University of Chicago Press.

Bess, J. L., and Webster, D. (Eds.). (1999). *Foundations of American higher education: An ASHE reader* (2nd ed.). Needham Heights, MA: Ginn.

Blackburn, R., and Fox, T. (1976). The socialization of a medical school faculty. *Journal of Medical Education, 51*(10), 806–817.

Blackwell, J. E. (1987). *Mainstreaming outsiders: The production of black professionals* (2nd ed.). Dix Hills, NJ: General Hall.

Bledstein, B. (1976). *The culture of professionalism: The middle class and the development of higher education in America.* New York: Norton.

Bomotti, S. (1994). Teaching assistant attitudes toward college teaching. *Review of Higher Education, 17*(4), 371–393.

Borawski, E. (1987). Graduate education: A bridge between two worlds. *American Sociologist, 18*(1), 79–82.

Bowen, W. G., and Rudenstine, N. L., with Sosa, J. A., Lord, G., Witte, M. L., and Turner, S. E. (1992). *In pursuit of the PhD.* Princeton, NJ: Princeton University Press.

Boyd, F. (1989). Developing presentation skills: A perspective from professional education. *English for Specific Purposes, 8*(3), 195–203.

Bragg, A. K. (1976). *The socialization process in higher education.* ERIC/AAHE Research Report, no. 7. Washington, DC: American Association for Higher Education.

Breneman, D. W. (1975). *Graduate school adjustments to the "new depression" in higher education.* Technical Report no. 3. Washington, DC: National Board on Graduate Education.

Brim, O. G., Jr. (1966). Socialization through the life cycle. In O. G. Brim, Jr., and S. Wheeler (Eds.), *Socialization after childhood: Two essays* (pp. 1–49). New York: Wiley.

Brown, E. R. (1970). *Professional orientations of graduate students and determinants of membership in the Graduate Students' Union at University of California.* Final report. Berkeley, CA: Center for Research and Development in Higher Education.

Brown, R., and Krager, L. (1985). Ethical issues in graduate education: Faculty and student responsibilities. *Journal of Higher Education, 56*(4), 403–418.

Bucher, R., and Stellings, J. (1977). *Becoming a professional.* London: Sage.

Bullis, C., and Bach, B. (1989). *Socialization turning points: An examination of change in organizational identification.* Paper presented at the annual meeting of the Western Speech Communication Association, Spokane, WA. (ED 306 607)

Burrell, G., and Morgan, G. (1979). *Sociological paradigms and organizational analysis.* Portsmouth, NH: Heinemann.

Bush, D., and Simmons, R. G. (1981). Socialization process over the life course. In M. Rosenberg and R. Turner (Eds.), *Social psychology: Sociological perspectives* (pp. 133–164). New York: Basic Books.

Cahn, S. (1986). *Saints and scamps.* Totowa, NJ: Rowman & Littlefield.

Caplovitz, D. (1980). *Student-faculty relations in medical school: A study of professional socialization.* New York: Arno Press.

Cardozier, V. (1991). *Should every professor be a researcher?* Higher Education Series Topical Paper 9101. (ED 328 162)

Carroll, J. (1971). Structured effects of professional schools on professional socialization: The case of protestant clergymen. *Social Forces, 50*(1), 61–74.

Chickering, A. W., and Reisser, L. (1993). *Education and identity* (2nd ed.). San Francisco: Jossey-Bass.

Clark, S., and Corcoran, M. (1986). Perspectives on the professional socialization of women faculty. *Journal of Higher Education, 57*(1), 20–43.

Clausen, J. A. (1968). Introduction. In J. A. Clausen (Ed.), *Socialization and Society* (pp. 1–17). Boston: Little, Brown.

Cockrell, K., Caplow, J., and Donaldson, J. (2000). A context for learning: Collaborative groups in the problem-based learning environment. *Review of Higher Education, 23*(3), 347–364.

Committee on Science, Engineering, and Public Policy. (1995). *Reshaping the graduate education of scientists and engineers.* Washington, DC: National Academy Press. (http://www.nap.edu/readingroom/books/grad)

Committee on Science, Engineering, and Public Policy. (1997). *Adviser, teacher, role model: On being a mentor to students in science and engineering.* Washington, DC: National Academy Press. (http://www.nap.edu/readingroom/books/mentor)

Coombs, R. H. (1978). *Mastering medicine: Professional socialization in medical school.* New York: Free Press.

Creamer, E., and McGuire, S. (1998). Applying the cumulative advantage perspective to scholarly writers in higher education. *Review of Higher Education, 22*(1), 73–82.

Daresh, J., and Playko, M. (1995). *Alternative career formation perspectives: Lessons for educational leadership from law, medicine, and training for the priesthood.* Paper presented at the annual meeting of the University Council for Educational Administration, Salt Lake City, UT. (ED 387 909)

Davis, W., and Minnis, D. (1993). Designing a program to prepare graduate students for careers as college teachers. *Innovative Higher Education, 17*(3), 211–224.

de Geus, A. (1997). *The living community.* Boston: Harvard Business School Press.

Duster, T. (1987). Graduate education at Berkeley. *American Sociologist, 18*(1), 83–86.

Egan, J. M. (1989). Graduate school and the self: A theoretical view of some negative effects of professional socialization. *Teaching Sociology, 17*(2), 200–217.

Epstein, C. F. (1970). *Women's place: Options and limits in professional careers.* Berkeley: University of California Press.

Epstein, C. F. (1993). *Women in law.* (2nd ed.). Urbana: University of Illinois Press.

Erikson, E. (1968). *Identity, youth, and crisis.* New York: Norton.

Feldman, S. (1974). *Escape from the doll's house: Women in graduate and professional education.* New York: McGraw-Hill.

Folse, K. (1991). Ethics and the profession: Graduate student training. *Teaching Sociology, 19*(3), 344–350.

Forsyth, P., and Danisiewicz, T. (1985). Toward theories of professionalization. *Work and Occupations, 12*(3), 59–76.

Gallagher, K., Hossler, D., Catania, F., and Kolman, E. (1986). *Personal and organizational factors affecting faculty productivity: The socialization process in graduate school.* Paper presented at the annual meeting of the Association for the Study of Higher Education, San Antonio, TX. (ED 268 895)

Gatz, L., and Hirt, J. (2000). Academic and social integration in cyberspace: Students and email. *Review of Higher Education, 23*(3), 299–318.

Geer, B. (1966). Occupational commitment and the teaching profession. *School Review, 74,* 31–47.

Geltner, B. (1994). The power of structural and symbolic redesign: Creating a collaborative learning community in higher education. (ED 374 757)

Getzels, J. (1963). Conflict and role behavior in an educational setting. In W. Charters, Jr., and N. Gage (Eds.), *Readings in the social psychology of education* (pp. 309–318). Boston: Allyn & Bacon.

Gilligan, C. (1978). *In a different voice: Psychological theory and women's development.* Cambridge, MA: Harvard University Press.

Goldberger, M. L., Maher, B. A., and Flattau, P. E. (Eds.). (1995). *Research-doctorate programs in the United States: Continuity and change.* Washington, DC: National Academy Press.

Golde, C. (2000). Should I stay or should I go? Student descriptions of the doctoral attrition process. *Review of Higher Education, 23*(4), 199–228.

Goodchild, L. F., Green, K. E., Katz, E. L., and Kluever, R. C. (Eds.). (1997). *Rethinking the dissertation process: Tackling personal and institutional obstacles.* New Directions for Higher Education, no. 99. San Francisco: Jossey-Bass.

Gottlieb, D. (1961). Processes of socialization in American graduate schools. *Social Forces, 40*(2), 124–131.

Griffith, E., and Delgado, A. (1979). On the professional socialization of black residents in psychiatry. *Journal of Medical Education, 54*(6), 471–476.

Gumport, P., and Chun, M. (1999). Technology and higher education: Opportunities and challenges for the new era. In P. Altbach, R. Berdahl, and P. Gumport (Eds.), *American Higher Education in the Twenty-First Century* (pp. 370–395). Baltimore: Johns Hopkins University Press.

Haas, J., and Shaffir, W. (1987). *Becoming doctors: The adoption of a cloak of competence.* Greenwich, CT: JAI Press.

Hafferty, F., and Franks, R. (1994). The hidden curriculum, ethics teaching, and the structure of medical education. *Academic Medicine, 69*(11), 861–871.

Haworth, J., and Conrad, C. (1997). *Emblems of quality in higher education: Developing and sustaining high quality programs.* Boston: Allyn & Bacon.

Helgesen, S. (1995). *The web of inclusion.* New York: Currency Doubleday.

Hill, M. (1973). *The religious order.* London: Heinemann Educational Books.

Hockin, R. (1981). *Symbiosis and socialization: A sociological examination of Ph.D. advising.* Ph.D. dissertation, University of Minnesota.

Hurtado, S., Milem, J., Clayton-Pedersen, A., and Allen, W. (1999). *Enacting diverse learning environments: Improving the climate for racial/ethnic diversity in higher education.* ASHE-ERIC Higher Education Report, vol. 26, no. 8. Washington, DC: The George Washington University, Graduate School of Education and Human Development.

Johnson, D. (1983). *Physicians in the making.* San Francisco: Jossey-Bass.

Jones, C. (1991). Campus wide and departmental orientations: The best of both worlds? In J. Nyquist, R. Abbott, D. Wulff, and J. Sprague (Eds.), *Preparing the professorate of tomorrow to teach* (pp. 135–141). Dubuque, IA: Kendall/Hunt.

Kanter, R. M. (1968). *Men and women of the corporation.* New York: Basic Books.

Katz, J., and Hartnett, R. (Eds.). (1976). *Scholars in the making.* Cambridge, MA: Ballinger.

Kay, S. (1978). Socializing the future elite: The nonimpact of a law school. *Social Science Quarterly, 59*(2), 347–354.

Keenan, C., Brown, G., Pontell, H., and Geis, G. (1985). Medical students' attitudes on physical fraud and abuse in the medicare and medicaid programs. *Journal of Medical Education, 60*(3), 167–173.

Kerckhoff, S. (1976). The status attainment process: Socialization or allocation. *Social Forces. 55*(2), 368–481.

Kerlin, S. (1995a). Pursuit of the Ph.D.: "Survival of the fittest," or is it time for a new approach? *Educational Policy Analysis Archives, 3*(16), 1–29. (http://olam.ed.asu.edu/epaa/v3n16.html)

Kerlin, S. (1995b). Surviving the doctoral years: Critical perspectives. *Educational Policy Analysis Archives, 3*(17), 1–37. (http://olam.ed.asu.edu/epaa/v3n17.html)

Ketefian, S. (1993). Essentials of doctoral education: Organization of programs around knowledge areas. *Journal of Professional Nursing, 9*(5), 255–261.

Killingsworth, R., and Twale, D. (1993). Integrating ethics into technical curricula. *Journal of Professional Issues in Engineering Education and Practice, 120*(1), 58–69.

Kirk, D., and Todd-Mancillas, W. (1991). Turning points in graduate student socialization: Implications for recruiting future faculty. *Review of Higher Education, 14*(3), 407–422.

Knight, J. (1973). *Medical students: Doctors in the making.* New York: Appleton-Century-Crofts.

Kuh, G. D., and Whitt, E. J. (1988). *The invisible tapestry: Culture in American colleges and universities.* ASHE-ERIC Higher Education Report, no. 1. Washington, DC: Association for the Study of Higher Education.

Kulik, J. (1985). *Using student ratings in evaluating teaching assistants.* Paper presented at the annual meeting of the American Educational Research Association, Chicago, IL. (ED 266 742)

Kyvik, S., and Smeby, J.-C. (1994). Teaching and research: The relationship between the supervision of graduate students and faculty research performance. *Higher Education, 28*(2), 227–239.

LaPidus, J. (1977). The outcome of graduate programs: A question of values. *American Journal of Pharmaceutical Education, 41*(4), 370–374.

Leatherman, C. (2001, February 9). The number of new Ph.D.'s drops for the first time since 1985. *Chronicle of Higher Education, 47*(22), A10–A11.

Leserman, J. (1981). *Men and women in medical school: How they change and how they compare.* New York: Praeger.

Levinson, D. J. (1978). *The seasons of a man's life.* New York: Knopf.

Lincoln, Y. (2000). When research is not enough: Community, care, and love. *Review of Higher Education, 23*(3), 241–256.

Lopate, C. (1968). *Women in medicine.* Baltimore: Johns Hopkins University Press.

Lortie, D. (1975). *School-teacher: A sociological study.* Chicago: University of Chicago Press.

Manis, J., and Meltzer, B. (1968). *Symbolic interaction: A reader in social psychology.* Boston: Allyn & Bacon.

Mann, K. (1994). Educating medical students: Lessons from research in continuing education. *Academic Medicine, 69*(1), 41–47.

Manzo, D., and Ross-Gordon, J. (1990). *Socialization outcomes of parttime graduate professional social work education: A comparison of adult students in career transition to social work with returning adult students who have undergraduate training and practical experience in social work.* (ED 372 724)

Marincovich, M., Prostko, J., and Stout, F. (Eds.). (1998). *The professional development of graduate teaching assistants.* Bolton, MA: Anker.

Mario, M. (1997). *Professional socialization of university lecturers in Mozambique.* Ph.D. dissertation, University of Pittsburgh.

McFarland, R., and Caplow, J. (1995). *Faculty perspectives of doctoral persistence within arts and sciences disciplines.* Paper presented at the annual meeting of the Association for the Study of Higher Education, Orlando, FL. (ED 391 422)

Merton, R. K., Reader, G., and Kendall, P. L. (1957). *The student physician.* Cambridge, MA: Harvard University Press.

Miller, G. A., and Wagner, L. W. (1971). Adult socialization. *Administrative Science Quarterly, 16,* 151–163.

Miller, S. (1966). Exchange and negotiated learning in graduate medical education. *Sociological Quarterly, 7,* 469–479.

Moller, G. (1998). Relationships. In R. van der Bogert (Ed.), *Making Learning Community Work* (pp. 41–50). New Directions for School Leadership, no. 7. San Francisco: Jossey-Bass.

Moore, W. E., and Rosenbloom, G. W. (1970). *The professions: Roles and rules.* New York: Russell Sage Foundation.

Mortimer, J. T., and Simmons, R. G. (1978). Adult socialization. *Annual Review of Sociology, 4,* 421–454.

Muse, W. V., Jr. (1999). *A study of faculty's perceptions of worker alienation and degree of favorability toward learning organization theory.* Ph.D. dissertation, Auburn University.

Myers, S. (1995). *Exploring the assimilation stage of GTA socialization: A preliminary investigation.* Paper presented at the annual meeting of the Speech Communication Association, San Antonio, TX. (ED 389 016)

Nalbandian, J. (1980). Teaching graduate students in public administration. *Teaching Political Science, 7*(2), 231–240.

Nerad, M., and Cerny, J. (1999). Widening the circle: Another look at women graduate students. *Communicator, 32*(6), 1–7. (http://www.cgsnet.org/PublicationsPolicyRes/ Communicatorpdfs/comm_backissues.htm)

Newman, M. (1994). A response to understanding transformation theory. *Adult Education Quarterly, 44*(4), 236–242.

Norris, C., and Barnett, B. (1994). *Cultivating a new leadership paradigm: From cohorts to community.* Paper presented at the annual meeting of the University Council for Educational Administration, Philadelphia, PA. (ED 387 877)

Norris, C., Basom, M., Barnett, B., and Yerkes, D. (1996). *The cohort: A vehicle for building transformational leadership skills.* Paper presented at the annual meeting of the American Educational Research Association, New York, NY.

Ohmann, R. (1990). Graduate students, professionals, intellectuals. *College English, 52*(3), 247–257.

Oleson, V. L., and Whittaker, E. (1968). *The silent dialogue: A study of the social psychology of professional socialization.* San Francisco: Jossey-Bass.

Oller, C. S. (1979). *Differential experiences of male and female aspirants in public school administration: A closer look at perceptions within the field.* Paper presented at the annual meeting of the American Educational Research Association, San Francisco, CA. (ED 173 932)

Olmsted, A., and Paget, M. (1969). Some theoretical issues in professional socialization. *Journal of Medical Education, 44*(8), 663–669.

Olsen, D., and Crawford, L. A. (1998). A five-year study of junior faculty expectations about their work. *Review of Higher Education, 22*(1), 39–54.

Ondrack, D. A. (1975). Socialization in professional schools. *Administrative Science Quarterly, 20*(1), 91–103.

Ortiz, F. I., and Marshall, C. (1988). Women in educational administration. In N. J. Boyan (Ed.), *Handbook of research on educational administration* (pp. 123–142). New York: Longman.

O'Toole, J. (1996). *Forming the future: Lessons from the Saturn Corporation.* Cambridge, MA: Blackwell Publishers.

Pascarella, E. T., and Terenzini, P. T. (1991). *How college affects students.* San Francisco: Jossey-Bass.

Pavalko, R., and Holley, J. (1974). Determinants of a professional self concept among graduate students. *Social Science Quarterly, 55*(2), 462–477.

Pease, J. (1967). Faculty influence and professional participation of doctoral students. *Sociological Inquiry, 37*(1), 63–70.

Platt, L., and Branch, R. (1972). *Innovation and the professionalization process: An analysis of dental education.* Paper presented at the annual meeting of the Southern Sociological Society, New Orleans, LA. (ED 061 878)

Porter, L. (1997). *Creating the virtual classroom: Distance learning with the Internet.* New York: Wiley.

Portes, A., and MacLeod, D. (1996). Educational progress of children of immigrants: The roles of class, ethnicity, and school context. *Sociology of Education, 69*(4), 255–275.

Privateer, P. M. (1999). Academic technology and the future of higher education: Strategic paths taken and not taken. *Journal of Higher Education, 22*(1), 39–54.

Pruitt-Logan, A. S., and Isaac, P. D. (Eds.). (1995). *Student services for the changing graduate student population.* New Directions for Student Services, no. 72. San Francisco: Jossey-Bass.

Quarantelli, E., Helfrich. M., and Yutsy, D. (1964). Faculty and student perceptions in a professional school. *Sociology and Social Research, 49*(1), 32–34.

Reinharz, S. (1979). *On becoming a social scientist.* Beverly Hills, CA: Sage.

Renn, K. (2000). Patterns of situational identity among biracial and multiracial college students. *Review of Higher Education, 23*(4), 399–420.

Ronkowski, S. (1989). *Changes in teaching assistant concerns over time.* Paper presented at the National Conference on the Training and Employment of Teaching Assistants, Seattle, WA. (ED 315 012)

Ronkowski, S., and Iannaccone, L. (1989). *Socialization research in administration, graduate school, and other professionals: The heuristic power of Van Gennep and Becker models.* Paper presented at the annual meeting of the American Educational Research Association, San Francisco, CA. (ED 306 489)

Rosen, B., and Bates, A. (1967). The structure of socialization in graduate school. *Sociological Inquiry, 37*(1), 71–84.

Rossman, M. (1995). *Negotiating graduate school: A guide for graduate students.* Thousand Oaks, CA: Sage.

Ryan, B. (1987). Graduate education in an age of decline. *American Sociologist, 18*(1), 63–68.

Scheurich, J., and Laible, J. (1995). The buck stops here in our preparation programs: Educative leadership for all children. *Educational Administration Quarterly, 31*(2), 313–322.

Sells, L. (1975). *Sex and discipline differences in professional socialization.* Paper presented at the annual meeting of the American Educational Research Association, Washington, DC. (ED 108 077)

Senge, P. M. (1990). *The fifth discipline: The art and practice of the learning organization.* New York: Doubleday.

Shannon, D., Twale, D., and Moore, M. (1998). Graduate teaching assistants' perceptions of their teaching effectiveness. *Journal of Higher Education, 69*(4), 440–466.

Shapiro, N. S., and Levine, J. H. (1999). *Creating learning communities: A practical guide to winning support, organizing for change, and implementing programs.* San Francisco: Jossey-Bass.

Sheehy, G. (1977). *Passages.* New York: Bantam Books.

Sheridan, J. 1991. A proactive approach to graduate teaching assistants in the research university: One graduate dean's perspective. In J. Nyquist, R. Abbott, D. Wulff, and J. Sprague (Eds.), *Preparing the Professorate of Tomorrow to Teach* (pp. 24–28). Dubuque, IA: Kendall/Hunt.

Sherlock, B., and Morris, R. 1967. The evolution of the professional: A paradigm. *Sociological Inquiry, 37*(1), 27–46.

Short, P., and Twale, D. (1994). Focus on instruction. In T. Mulkeen and N. Cambron-McCabe (Eds.), *Democratic leadership: The changing context of administrative presentation* (pp. 133–144). New York: Ablex.

Slawski, C. (1973). *Professional socialization in organizational context: Hypotheses and comparative cases.* Paper presented at the annual meeting of the American Psychological Association, New York. (ED 157 451)

Slevin, J. (1992). *The next generation: Preparing graduate students for the professional responsibilities of college teachers.* Washington, DC: Association of American Colleges. (ED 353 884)

Smart, J. C., Feldman, K. A., and Ethington, C. A. (2000). *Academic disciplines: Holland's theory and the study of college students and faculty.* Nashville, TN: Vanderbilt University Press.

Smith, K. (1993). A case study on the successful development of an international teaching assistant. *Innovative Higher Education, 17*(3), 149–163.

Sprague, J., and Nyquist, J. (1989). TA supervision. In J. Nyquist, R. Abbott, and D. Wulff (Eds.), *Teaching assistant training in the 1990s.* New Directions for Teaching and Learning, no. 39. San Francisco: Jossey-Bass.

Stark, J. S. (1998). Classifying professional preparation programs. *Journal of Higher Education, 69*(4), 353–383.

Stark, J. S., Lowther, M., and Hagerty, B. (1986). *Responsive professional education: Balancing outcomes and opportunities.* ASHE/ERIC Higher Education Report, no. 3. Washington, DC: Association for the Study of Higher Education.

Stark, J. S., Lowther, M., Hagerty, B., and Orczyk, C. (1986). A conceptual framework for the study of preservice professional programs in colleges and universities. *Journal of Higher Education, 57*(3), 231–258.

Staton, A. (1990). *Communication and student socialization.* Norwood, NJ: Ablex.

Staton, A., and Darling, A. (1989). Socialization of teaching assistants. In J. Nyquist, R. Abbott, and D. Wulff (Eds.), *Teaching Assistant Training in the 1990s* (pp. 15–22). New Directions for Teaching and Learning, no. 39. San Francisco: Jossey-Bass.

Stein, E. L. (1992). *Socialization at a protestant seminary.* Ph.D. dissertation, University of Pittsburgh.

Stein, E. L., and Weidman, J. C. (1989). *Socialization in graduate school: A conceptual framework.* Paper presented at the annual meeting of the Association for the Study of Higher Education, Atlanta, GA.

Stein, E. L., and Weidman. J. C. (1990). *The socialization of doctoral students to academic norms.* Paper presented at the annual meeting of the American Educational Research Association, Boston, MA.

Stover, R. (1989). *Making it and breaking it: The fate of public interest commitment during law school.* Urbana: University of Illinois Press.

Sullivan, T. (1991). The shimming effect: Why good graduate students are unprepared for the professorate of tomorrow. In J. Nyquist, R. Abbott, D. Wulff, and J. Sprague (Eds.), *Preparing the professorate of tomorrow to teach* (pp. 17–23). Dubuque, IA: Kendall/Hunt.

Thielens, W., Jr. (1980). *The socialization of law students: A case study in three parts.* New York: Arno Press.

Thompson, M. (1978). *Graduate school: Pursuit of truth or delicate hustle?* (ED 165 586)

Thompson, M. (Ed.). (1998). Distance learning in higher education. In C. C. Gibson (Ed.), *Distance learning in higher education* (pp. 9–24). Madison, WI: Atwood.

Thornton, R., and Nardi, P. M. (1975). The dynamics of role acquisition. *American Journal of Sociology, 80*(4), 870–885.

Tierney, W. G. (1997). Organizational socialization in higher education. *Journal of Higher Education, 68*(1), 1–16.

Tierney, W. G., and Bensimon, E. (1996). *Promotion and tenure: Community and socialization in academe.* Albany: SUNY Press.

Tierney, W. G., and Rhoads, R. A. (1994). *Faculty socialization as cultural process: A mirror of institutional commitment.* ASHE-ERIC Higher Education Report, no. 93–6. Washington, DC: The George Washington University, School of Education and Human Development.

Tinto, V. (1993). *Leaving college: Rethinking the causes and cures of student attrition* (2nd ed.). Chicago: University of Chicago Press.

Turner, C.S.V., Myers, S. L., Jr., and Creswell, J. W. (1999). Exploring underrepresentation: The case of faculty of color in the midwest. *Journal of Higher Education, 70*(1), 27–59.

Turner, C.S.V., and Thompson, J. (1993). Socializing women doctoral students: Minority and majority experiences. *Review of Higher Education, 16*(3), 355–370.

Twale, D., Douvanis, C., and Sekula. F. (1992). Affirmative action strategies and professional schools: Case illustrations of exemplary programs. *Higher Education, 24*(2), 177–192.

Twale, D., and Kochan, F. (1998). *Using cohorts to create a learning community in an educational leadership program.* Paper presented at the annual meeting of the Eastern Educational Research Association, Tampa, FL.

Twale, D., and Kochan, F. (1999). Restructuring an educational leadership program: The teacup adventure. *International Studies in Educational Administration, 27*(1), 61–69.

Twale, D., and Kochan, F. (2000). Assessment of an alternative cohort model for part-time students in an educational leadership program. *Journal of School Leadership, 10,* 188–208.

Twale, D., Kochan, F., and Reed, C. (1999). *Creating collaboration and community in doctoral leadership programs.* Roundtable presented at the annual meeting of the Eastern Educational Research Association, Hilton Head, SC.

Twale, D., Kochan, F., and Reed, C. (2000). *How are educational leadership programs creating collaborative communities?* Paper presented at the annual meeting of the Eastern Educational Research Association, Clearwater, FL.

Twale, D., Shannon, D., and Moore, M. (1997). NGTAs and IGTAs training and experience: Comparisons between self-ratings and undergraduate student evaluations. *Innovative Higher Education, 22*(1), 61–77.

University of Michigan, Rackham Graduate School. (2000a). *How to get the mentoring you want: A guide for graduate students at a diverse university.* (http://www.rackham.umich.edu/StudentInfo/Publications/index.html)

University of Michigan, Rackham Graduate School. (2000b). *How to mentor graduate students: A guide for faculty at a diverse university.* (http://www.rackham.umich.edu/StudentInfo/Publications/index.html)

Valverde, L. A., and Brown, F. (1988). Influences on leadership development among racial and ethnic minorities. In N. J. Boyan (Ed.), *Handbook of research on educational administration* (pp. 143–158). New York: Longman.

Van Maanen, J., and Schein, E. (1979). Toward a theory of organizational socialization. In B. M. Straw (Ed.), *Research in organizational behavior,* (pp. 209–264).Greenwich, CT: JAI Press.

Wallace, S. (1966). Reference group behavior in occupational role socialization. *Sociological Quarterly, 7,* 366–372.

Weidman, J. C. (1989a). Undergraduate socialization: A conceptual approach. In J. C. Smart (Ed.), *Higher education: Handbook of theory and research* (Vol. 5, pp. 289–322). New York: Agathon.

Weidman, J. C. (1989b). The world of higher education: A socialization-theoretical perspective. In K. Hurrelmann and U. Engel (Eds.), *The social world of adolescents: International perspectives* (pp. 87–105). Berlin: de Gruyter.

Weinholtz, D. (1991). The socialization of physicians during attending rounds: A study of team learning among medical students. *Qualitative Health Research, 1*(2), 152–177.

Welton, M. (1993). The contribution of critical theory to our understanding of adult learning. In S. Merriam (Ed.), *An update on adult learning theory* (pp. 81–90). New Directions for Adult and Continuing Education, no. 57. San Francisco: Jossey-Bass.

Wentworth, W. M. (1980). *Context and understanding: An inquiry into socialization theory.* New York: Elsevier.

Wheeler, S. (1966). The structure of formally organized socialization settings. In O. G. Brim, Jr., and S. Wheeler (Eds.), *Socialization after childhood: Two essays* (pp. 51–116). New York: Wiley.

Wilkening, L. (1991). Teaching assistants for the professorate. In J. Nyquist, R. Abbott, D. Wulff, and J. Sprague (Eds.), *Preparing the professorate of tomorrow to teach* (pp. 12–16). Dubuque, IA: Kendall/Hunt.

Willie, C. V., Grady, M. K., and Hope, R. O. (1991). *African-Americans and the doctoral experience: Implications for policy.* New York: Columbia University, Teachers College Press.

Wolensky, R. (1976). *Professional confidence and the graduate student's double bind.* Paper presented at the annual meeting of American Sociological Association, New York. (ED 138 525)

Wright, C. (1967). Changes in the occupational commitment of graduate sociology students: A research note. *Sociological Inquiry, 37*(1), 55–62.

Yoder, J. (1984). *Surviving the transition from graduate student to assistant professor.* Paper presented at the annual meeting of the American Psychological Association, Toronto, ON. (ED 249 867)

Zeller, N. (1995). Distance education and public policy. *Review of Higher Education, 18*(1), 123–148.

Index

Collaborative plan model: core elements and, 29t; overview of, 27–28f
Collective socialization, 7
Columbia Law School study, 58
Commitment: collaborative approach to, 29t; credentialism vs., 85; functional approach to, 22t–23t; interactive approach to, 37f; professional social order and, 20–21; structural engagement and, 85–87; three types of, 19–20
Communication (formal socialization), 13
Competence, 85–87
Conrad, C., 93
Coombs, R. H., 5, 48, 62, 73, 81
Corcoran, M., 12, 13
Crawford, L. A., 86
Creamer, E., 86
Credentialism, 85
Creswell, J. W., 42, 43, 44, 93, 94, 95, 96, 99
Cumulative advantage, 86

D

Danisiewicz, T., 51
Daresh, J., 6, 65, 66, 71, 76, 85, 92
Darling, A., 3, 13, 14, 62, 63, 70, 79, 80
Davis, W., 77, 79
de Geus, A., 92
Delgado, A., 44, 45
Demings total quality management, 26
Dental student self-image, 74
Discipline pecking order, 57
Disjunctive socialization, 8
Dissertations: challenges of writing, 75; in natural sciences, 81
Distance learning, 51–53
Diverse graduate student population: current state of, 41–42; increasing the, 93–94
Divestiture, 8–9
Donaldson, J., 95
Doolittle, Eliza (*My Fair Lady* character), 5
Douvanis, C., 94

E

Egan, J. M., 20, 47
Epstein, C. F., 33, 42, 58
Erikson, E., 64
Ethical professional principles, 51
Ethington, C. A., 109

F

Faculty: nonlinear models role of, 26–30; relationship with graduate assistants, 79; as role models for minority students, 46; Standard Plan model role of, 25–26; student confirming to ideology of, 60;

technology impact on role of, 52–53. *See also* Mentors
Faculty role/expectations: investment and, 66–69; involvement and, 75–79; knowledge acquisition and, 58–62; modifying, 98–100
Feedback (New Plan model), 26–27f
Feldman, K. A., 33
Fixed pace, 7
Flattau, P. E., 57
Folse, K., 51
Formal socialization process, 7
Formal socialization stage: core elements/collaborative approach to, 29t; core elements/functional approach to, 22t–23t; described, 12–13
Forsyth, P., 51
Fox, T., 50, 58
Franks, R., 48, 81

G

Gallagher, K., 59
Garrison, D., 52, 53, 97
Gatz, L., 53
Geer, B., 17, 18, 20, 51, 57, 61, 69, 73, 74, 81
Geis, G., 51
Geltner, B., 92
Gender differences: North Carolina medical school study on, 44; overview of, 45–46
Getzels, J., 31, 34, 35
Gilligan, C., 32, 33
Goldberger, M. L., 57
Golde, C., 26, 95, 96
Goodchild, L. F., 97
Gottlieb, D., 15, 77, 78
Graduate assistants: expanding opportunities for, 98–99; expected outcomes of, 79–81; faculty relations with, 78–79; supervised practice by, 76–77
Graduate education: changes in institutions of, 9; diversity in, 41–46; ethical principles learned in, 51; impact of technology/distance learning on, 51–53; modifying faculty/administrative role in, 98–100; offering additional student support during, 94–98; recommendations for improving support in, 99–100; research interest enhancing, 78; socialization of, 91–93. *See also* Academic program differences
Graduate students: diverse population of, 41–46; international, 46–47; mentors and socialization of, 8; modifying faculty relationship with, 98–100; nonlinear models role of, 26–30; offering additional support to, 94–98; organizational structures for, 71–73;

peer culture of, 62–63; program structures and, 74; recommendations for improving support of, 99–100; self-image stereotypes of, 74; during socialization stages, 11–15; socialization and success of, 2–3; Standard Plan model role of, 25–26; structural engagement by, 19–21; technology impact on role of, 52; various experiences by, 2. *See also* Novices

Grady, M. K., 44, 96

Green, K. E., 97

Griffith, E., 44, 45

Gumport, P., 52

H

Haas, J., 61

Hafferty, F., 48, 81

Hagerty, B., 9, 15, 31, 56, 65

Hartnett, R., 34

Haworth, J., 93

Helfrich, M., 48, 69, 74

Helgesen, S., 92

Hill, M., 71

Hirt, J., 53

Hockin, R., 50, 67, 80, 83

Holley, J., 49, 62, 71

Hope, R. O., 44, 96

Hossler, D., 59

Hughes, E. C., 18, 51, 57, 61, 69, 73, 74, 81

Humanities students: assistantships among, 77; professionalism outcomes for, 81

Hurtado, S., 35, 43

I

Iannaccone, L., 16, 19, 44, 50, 79

Identity. *See* Role identity

Incumbents: knowledge acquisition and becoming, 16; personal stage and, 15

Individual socialization process, 7

Informal socialization process, 7

Informal socialization stage: core elements/collaborative approach to, 29t; core elements/functional approach to, 22t–23t; described, 14

Interactive frameworks: Bragg, 31–33; Stark, Lowther, Hagerty, Orczyk, 31; Stein and Weidman, 33–36; Weidman, 25, 30–31; Weidman, Twale, Stein, 36–40, 37f

Interactive stages of socialization, 36–40, 37f

International students, 46–47

Investiture, 8

Investment: collaborative approach to, 29t; described, 17–18, 63–64; functional approach to, 22t–23t; interactive approach to, 37f

Investment differences: in faculty role/expectations, 66–69; in organizational structures, 64–65; in professional standards, 65–66

Involvement: collaborative approach to, 29t; described, 18–19, 70–71; functional approach to, 22t–23t; interactive approach to, 37f

Involvement differences: in expected outcomes, 79–81; in faculty role in supervised practice, 75–79; in organizational structures, 71–73; in program structures, 73–75; of students with peers, 82–83

Involvement theory, 18

Isaac, P. D., 97

J

Johnson, D., 42

Jones, C., 78, 79

K

Kanter, R. M., 19, 20

Katz, E. L., 97

Katz, J., 34

Kay, S., 58

Keenan, C., 51

Kendall, P. L., 4, 15, 32

Kerckhoff, S., 34

Kerlin, S., 43, 45

Ketefian, S., 6, 86

Killingsworth, R., 51

Kirk, D., 62, 77, 80

Kluever, R. C., 97

Knight, J., 49, 74

Knowledge acquisition: collaborative approach to, 29t; described, 55–56; functional approach to, 22t–23t; interactive approach to, 37f; professional identity through, 19; socialization and, 16

Knowledge acquisition differences: in faculty role/supervision, 58–62; in organizational structures, 56–57; in program structures, 57–58; in student peer culture, 62–63

Kochan, F., 14, 15, 27, 70, 72, 82, 83, 95, 96, 97

Kolman, E., 59

Krager, L., 15, 67

Kuh, G. D., 35

Kulik, J., 46

Kyvik, S., 81

L

Laible, J., 92

LaPidus, J., 78, 80

Law students: clinical experiences of, 76; curricular content differences of, 58; ethics learned by, 51; organizational structures for, 72;

ASHE-ERIC
Higher Education Reports

The mission of the Educational Resources Information Center (ERIC) system is to improve American education by increasing and facilitating the use of educational research and information on practice in the activities of learning, teaching, educational decision making, and research, wherever and whenever these activities take place.

Since 1983, the ASHE-ERIC Higher Education Report series has been published in cooperation with the Association for the Study of Higher Education (ASHE). Starting in 2000, the series has been published by Jossey-Bass in conjunction with the ERIC Clearinghouse on Higher Education.

Each monograph is the definitive analysis of a tough higher education problem, based on thorough research of pertinent literature and institutional experiences. Topics are identified by a national survey. Noted practitioners and scholars are then commissioned to write the reports, with experts providing critical reviews of each manuscript before publication.

Six monographs in the series are published each year and are available on individual and subscription bases. To order, use the order form at the back of this issue.

Qualified persons interested in writing a monograph for the series are invited to submit a proposal to the National Advisory Board. As the preeminent literature review and issue analysis series in higher education, the Higher Education Reports are guaranteed wide dissemination and provide national exposure for accepted candidates. Execution of a monograph requires at least a minimal familiarity with the ERIC database, including *Resources in Education* and the current *Index to Journals in Education*. The objective of these reports is to bridge conventional wisdom and practical research.

Advisory Board

Susan Frost
Office of Institutional Planning and Research
Emory University

Kenneth Feldman
SUNY at Stony Brook

Anna Ortiz
Michigan State University

James Fairweather
Michigan State University

Lori White
Stanford University

Esther E. Gottlieb
West Virginia University

Carol Colbeck
Pennsylvania State University

Jeni Hart
University of Arizona

Review Panelists and Consulting Editors

Leonard Baird
Ohio State University

Nancy Gafney
Council for Graduate Schools

Ronald Lee
University of Nebraska

Jeffrey Milem
University of Maryland

Suzanne Ortega
University of Nebraska

Anne S. Pruitt-Logan
Council of Graduate Schools

John C. Smart
University of Memphis

Recent Titles

Volume 28 ASHE-ERIC Higher Education Reports

1. The Changing Nature of the Academic Deanship
   Mimi Wolverton, Walter H. Gmelch, Joni Montez, and Charles T. Nies

2. Faculty Compensation Systems: Impact on the Quality of Higher Education
   Terry P. Sutton, Peter J. Bergerson

Volume 27 ASHE-ERIC Higher Education Reports

1. The Art and Science of Classroom Assessment: The Missing Part of Pedagogy
   Susan M. Brookhart

2. Due Process and Higher Education: A Systemic Approach to Fair Decision Making
   Ed Stevens

3. Grading Students' Classroom Writing: Issues and Strategies
   Bruce W. Speck

4. Posttenure Faculty Development: Building a System for Faculty Improvement and Appreciation
   Jeffrey W. Alstete

5. Digital Dilemma: Issues of Access, Cost, and Quality in Media-Enhanced and Distance Education
   Gerald C. Van Dusen

6. Women and Minority Faculty in the Academic Workplace: Recruitment, Retention, and Academic Culture
   Adalberto Aguirre, Jr.

7. Higher Education Outside of the Academy
   Jeffrey A. Cantor

8. Academic Departments: How They Work, How They Change
   Barbara E. Walvoord, Anna K. Carey, Hoke L. Smith, Suzanne W. Soled, Philip K. Way, Debbie Zorn

Volume 26 ASHE-ERIC Higher Education Reports

Volume 25 ASHE-ERIC Higher Education Reports

Volume 24 ASHE-ERIC Higher Education Reports

Volume 23 ASHE-ERIC Higher Education Reports

Back Issue/Subscription Order Form

Copy or detach and send to:
Jossey-Bass, 350 Sansome Street, San Francisco CA 94104-1342

Call or fax toll free!
Phone 888-378-2537 6AM-5PM PST; Fax 800-605-2665

Individual
reports:

Please send me the following reports at $24 each
(Important: please include series initials and issue number, such as AEHE 27:1)

1. AEHE _____

_____

_____

$ _____ Total for individual reports

$ _____ Shipping charges (for individual reports *only;* subscriptions are exempt
from shipping charges): Up to $30, add $5^{50} • $30^{01}–$50, add $6^{50}
$50^{01}–$75, add $8 • $75^{01}–$100, add $10 • $100^{01}–$150, add $12
Over $150, call for shipping charge

Subscriptions

Please ❏ start my subscription to *ASHE-ERIC Higher Education
Reports* for the year <u>2001</u> at the following rate (6 issues):
U.S.: $108   Canada: $188   All others: $256

$ _____ Total individual reports and subscriptions (Add appropriate
sales tax for your state for individual reports. No sales tax on U.S.
subscriptions. Canadian residents, add GST for subscriptions and
individual reports.)

❏ Payment enclosed (U.S. check or money order only)

❏ VISA, MC, AmEx, Discover Card # _____ Exp. date _____

Signature _____ Day phone _____

❏ Bill me (U.S. institutional orders only. Purchase order required.)

Purchase order #_____

Federal Tax ID 135593032   GST 89102-8052

Name _____

Address _____

_____

Phone_____ E-mail _____

For more information about Jossey-Bass, visit our Web site at:
www.josseybass.com   **PRIORITY CODE = ND1**

John C. Weidman is professor of higher education and sociology at the University of Pittsburgh, where he has been since 1979. He is best known for his work on the socialization of undergraduates. Since the early 1990s, he has also been working on comparative higher education management and policy analysis. In addition to graduate teaching and research in these areas, he has consulted on projects in Mongolia, Laos, and South Africa. His visiting professorships include the UNESCO Chair of Higher Education Research at Maseno University College in Kenya and Fulbright Professor of the sociology of education at Augsburg University in Germany.

Darla J. Twale is professor of higher education administration at the University of Dayton. For eleven years before coming to Dayton, she was a faculty member in educational leadership at Auburn University. Early in her career, she developed a line of research in residence life; an additional area of research emerged that grew more broadly to include women students, faculty, and administrators. More recently, her research has focused on collaboration and community.

Elizabeth Leahy Stein is an independent scholar, substitute teacher, and antiques dealer. She has been an assoicate professor of nursing at South Dakota State University and a teaching fellow at the University of Pittsburgh.